Frommer's®

BRITAIN'S BEST
BIKE
RIDES

Macmillan ■ USA

Produced by AA Publishing

Consultant Editor: David Hancock
Design: ppd

Contributors: Chris Beeching, Pete and Lorraine Bird, Karl Briggs,
Brian Curtis, Victor K Douglas, Stuart Edinborough, Philip Ennis, Mike
Francis, David Hancock, Derek and Evelyn Hancock, Ron Healey, Alan
Hodgson, Billy McCormick, Alan Menzies, Richard Nicholl, Mike
Power, Arnold Robinson, Sheila Simpson, Iris Stevens, Ken Strong,
John Taylor, W J Teague, Maurice Truby, Les Wyle

Published in the United States by Macmillan Travel
A Simon & Schuster Macmillan Company
1633 Broadway, New York, NY 10019

Macmillan is a registered trademark of Macmillan, Inc.

The contents of this book are believed correct at the time of printing.
Nevertheless, the publishers cannot be held responsible for any errors
or omissions or for changes in the details given in this book or for the
consequences of any reliance on the information provided by the same.
We have tried to ensure accuracy in this book, but things do change
and we would be grateful if readers would advise us of any inaccuracies
they may encounter.

Colour separation by Fotographics Ltd
Printed and bound by Graficromo SA, Spain

Essential Information for Cyclists

THESE routes have been carefully researched, but despite our best efforts to ensure accuracy, changes may occur at any stage during the lifetime of the book. Please remember that roads are subject to reclassification, resulting in road numbers changing, and that construction of new bypasses may alter road junctions, signposting and traffic priorities. Off-road cycling conditions vary with the changing seasons: routes may become muddy in winter, or overgrown in summer.

All the rides have been devised to incorporate relatively traffic-free country lanes, designated cyclepaths, or good surfaced bridleways and by-ways. Inevitably, main roads have to be crossed or ridden for short stretches, so rules of the road must be observed, including the Highway Code. Ride in single file on narrow or busy roads, keep at least 3m away from other cyclists in wet weather, and take extra care on fast descents. Beware of loose gravel, and look and listen for fast traffic, especially on narrow lanes with blind bends. Always indicate your intentions clearly, and try to anticipate the behaviour of other road users.

Cycling off-road has its own code of conduct. You have no right to cycle on public footpaths, the only 'rights of way' open to cyclists being bridleways and unsurfaced by-ways, but you may meet other vehicles with access on by-ways. Look out for the waymarking arrows: yellow for footpaths, blue for bridleways, red for by-ways. Please give way to both walkers and horseriders, giving adequate warning of your approach. To avoid erosion, keep to the trail.

To guarantee extra safety when cycling, you should equip yourself and your bike adequately. Make sure your bike is in good working order, check your brakes, tyres and wheels and carry any luggage in panniers so that the bike is well balanced. Be seen: wear high visibility clothing and reflective strips, and carry lights at night. It is advisable to wear a safety helmet. Take sufficient food, water, extra clothing (especially a waterproof jacket), and carry essential spares and tools.

The rides, mostly circular trips, have been selected to take you through attractive and varied areas of the country, and to be enjoyable both for experienced and novice cycling families. The approximate distance is always stated. The detailed information box for each route indicates the difficulty of the ride, from 1 (easy) to 3 (challenging). If a route includes steep hills or demanding track cycling, we have highlighted this. Refreshment facilities are listed, but mention in this book does not imply AA inspection or recognition, although establishments may have an AA classification.

The National Grid reference for the start of each ride is given. These numbers relate to the grid squares on the larger scale Ordnance Survey maps (1:50,000), which cyclists may like to use in addition to the maps in this book. If you have to cut the ride short, or decide to make a detour, you will need such a map.

Remember the Country Code; in particular, please close gates behind you and do not discard litter. Guard against all risk of fire.

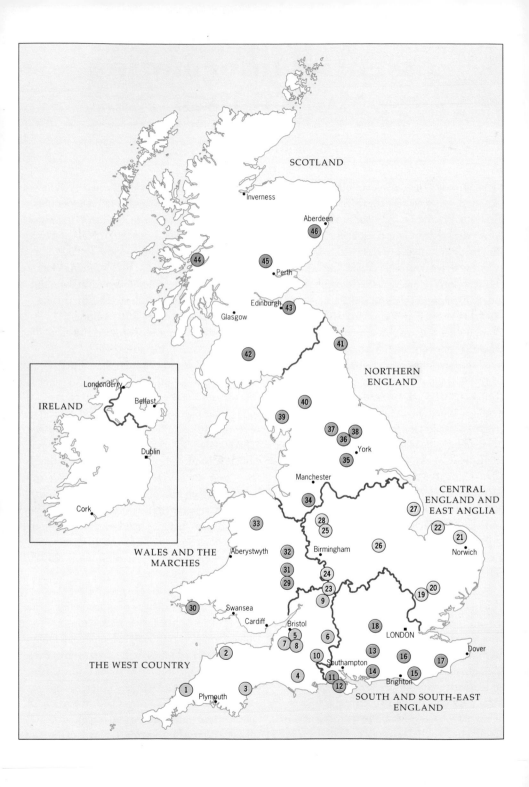

SCOTLAND

Inverness

Aberdeen
46

44

45   Perth

Edinburgh 43
Glasgow

42   41

IRELAND

Londonderry
Belfast

Dublin

Cork

NORTHERN
ENGLAND

40

39

37 38
36
35   York

Manchester

CENTRAL
ENGLAND AND
EAST ANGLIA

34

27

33

28
25

22
21
Norwich

WALES AND THE
MARCHES

Aberystwyth   32

Birmingham   26

31
29   24

23

30   9

Swansea

Cardiff   19   20

Bristol   18   LONDON

5   Dover

7   8   6

2   10   13

Southampton   16

4   14   17

1   Plymouth   3   11   15

12   Brighton

THE WEST COUNTRY

SOUTH AND SOUTH-EAST
ENGLAND

The Rides

The West Country

South and South-east England

Central England and East Anglia

Wales and the Marches

Northern England

Scotland

Why a Cycling Vacation?

If you've picked up this book, a blitzkrieg bus tour across Europe probably doesn't appeal to you. You'd rather set your own itinerary. You prefer a more active vacation, one that allows you to detour from congested tourist paths and get out on your own.

What better way to do that than on a bicycle? Cool air in your face, blood coursing through your veins, you'll meet locals from small towns and rural areas, not just fellow tourists stampeding from one greatest hit to the next. Following this guide, you can power your own way through the rolling English countryside—stopping off at picturesque villages and historic abbeys, or pedaling around beautiful national parks and nature reserves. Using the road as your guide, you'll be able to slow down and immerse

Cycling is a great way to explore the countryside

yourself in all the sights, sounds, and smells of Britain.

The 46 rides found in this book were originally designed for British cyclotourists who wanted to explore their own countryside at a leisurely pace. The rides range from 11 to 29 miles in length. Along with detailed maps and descriptions, we tell you precisely where to go, what to look for, where to rent a bike or get repairs, and where to find a bed and a meal.

You'll find no lung-busting climbs here, just gentle hills, country lanes, and quaint towns. The carefully selected and researched rides in this book are meant for individuals of all ages—novices as well as regular cyclists—who want a rewarding trip and enjoy a bit of exercise. A number of the rides are designed for the enjoyment of the whole family.

This guide makes it easy for you to design your vacation and cycle in Britain—according

to your interests and timetable. How you plan your trip is up to you.

Knobby tires and a sturdy frame mark the mountain bike (above) in contrast to the lighter hybrid (below)

Warming Up: Planning Essentials

How much do I have to ride? Choose a single ride, do several in a particular region, or do a number of rides in more than one part of Britain. Combine cycling with walking tours, or pack your panniers and set out to see the country by bike. Regardless of your interests, time, and abilities, you'll experience more of what you came to see, and you'll go home relaxed and rejuvenated, with fit legs and fond memories.

Where will I stay? Stay at country inns or base yourself in towns. Each ride description provides at least one local inn where you can stay after a day of cycling. For more information, consult a respected guidebook, such as *Frommer's England* or *Frommer's Scotland,* or log on to a few of the World Wide Web sites listed below that offer information on lodging throughout Britain. In town, check with the local tourist information center; the nearest one is cited in each ride description.

What about equipment? Take your own bicycle or rent one there; the choice depends mostly upon how much cycling you plan to do. (See "Road Gear," below, for a discussion of bikes and "Taking Your Own Bike—Or Renting One Abroad" for information about transporting your own.)

When should I go? Cycling in the U.K. is a seasonal activity; all but the most dedicated cyclists will probably want to avoid the months of November to March. But whether you go in late

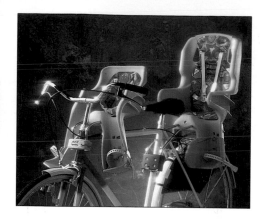

spring, summer, or early fall, you should find conditions good for cycling. Of course it's Britain, so you may not be able to avoid a bit of rain. No worry. Just duck into a local pub for a pint of English ale, or dry off and grab a spot of tea.

The Rides

Britain's Best Bike Rides are day trips that take you into the countryside, but never far from attractions, lodging, and places to eat and drink.

The rides range in distance from 11 to 29 miles. All have been devised to incorporate less-traveled country lanes, designated cyclepaths, or good, surfaced paths. Some feature gentle climbs while others include patches of optional off-road riding, but most are leisurely. All are rated by level of difficulty, from 1 (easy) to 3 (challenging). Any potentially difficult segments, whether hills or dirt paths, are detailed. Most are circular routes, so you won't be stuck seeing the same scenery on the return trip. You'll pedal on trails, alongside canals, through small towns, and even on old railway track, now ideal for cycling.

For each ride you have precise instructions—where to turn, landmarks to look for, and sights along the way—so you won't get lost or miss anything. Every ride description contains:

With a rental car and a rack, go anywhere

Take the whole family cycling

- A full-color, easy-to-read map with the route clearly plotted and all steep hills and difficult or offroad sections highlighted
- Total distance and rating ("grade")
- Where to go for visitor information
- Where to get a bite to eat, have tea, or down a pint to quench your thirst
- Where to stay in the area
- The location of the nearest railway station and bike shop for rentals and repairs
- Places of architectural, historic, and cultural interest
- "What to Look For"—insider tips in the area
- Color photographs of important sights along the way.

Planning Your Days: These rides have been carefully mapped out, but they will still require some planning on your part. Get an early start and be sure to allow ample time for pit stops; a leisurely lunch, whether a picnic or pub grub; and visits you wish to make along the way. Consult our description of the terrain for the day's ride: Is it a simple road ride or are there climbs or offroad sections that will demand more time? If there's a castle, historic house, museum, or park along the route, you should build time for it in your schedule.

Road Gear

Selecting a Bike: To do these rides, you'll probably want one of three types of bicycles: A standard **touring bike** has drop handlebars, narrow tires, and triple chainrings. A **mountain bike** is more durable, with wider, knobby tires and straight handlebars. And a **hybrid (or city) bike** is a cross between the two. If you plan on doing any offroad riding, a mountain bike is your best bet (although a hybrid may also suffice). Some of these are equipped with front suspension forks, or "shock absorbers," to lessen the blow of uneven terrain. Most recent versions of these bicycles come with 18 or 21 speeds and many have three chainrings, allowing you to ascend inclines with ease. If you plan to stick to well paved roads, a touring or hybrid bicycle will roll with the least resistance (although you can also outfit your mountain bike with "slick" tires for better road handling). Long distances on a heavy mountain bike with wide, knobby tires can be exhausting.

Any of these bicycles can be outfitted with a rack and panniers to carry gear.

Accessories: You should carry a few items with you, either in a fanny pack or an under-the-seat tool bag. These items, at a minimum, should include:

- Patch kit to repair flat tires
- Allen keys
- Tire levers
- Spare tube (make sure it's the right size for your bicycle)
- Screwdriver.

A cycling helmet is recommended for safety

Bright clothing will ensure that you are visible on the road

In addition, you (or at least one person in your group) should have a frame pump. Other items you won't want to forget include sunscreen, a first-aid kit, and sunglasses.

Clothing: You've seen the cycling clubs in their Technicolor, head-to-toe Lycra cycling gear. Do you need to look like them just to do some laid-back rides? Absolutely not, although technical gear such as padded spandex **cycling shorts,** padded fingerless **gloves,** and firm-soled **cycling shoes** will greatly enhance your comfort. Padded cycling shorts particularly are a good investment; they won't slide on your legs and crotch and cause irritation, and they are quick-drying for overnight laundering. Still, there's nothing wrong with very leisurely biking in shorts and tennis shoes.

A **helmet,** however, is essential. Accidents will happen, no matter how careful you are, and a good, ANSI/ASTM-certified helmet will protect your brain. You should never hop on a bike without a safety hat. Make sure that the helmet fits snugly. You can purchase an excellent helmet for less than $50; brands to look for include Bell, Giro, and Specialized. Bike rental shops should include helmets with your rental. If they don't, demand it or go elsewhere.

If the weather turns cool or rainy, you would be wise to carry a **lightweight jacket,** such as a pile fleece, and a waterproof **rain jacket.**

Water & Food Intake: You should attach water-bottle cages to your bike (or ask the bike rental shop to do so). Continual consumption of **water** during your ride (about 12 ounces per hour) is critical to replace lost body fluids. If you are unable to carry

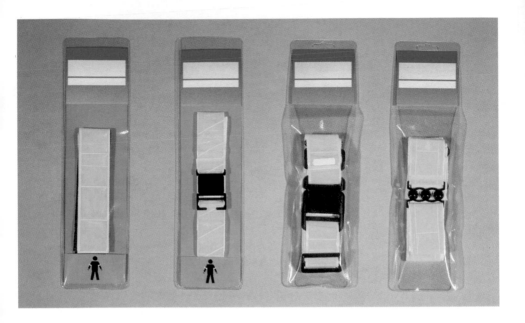

Reflective strips make night riding safer

water with you, make sure you stop frequently to drink fluids.

You should also carry **high-energy snack foods** that are high in carbohydrates. Frequent munching on bananas, cereal bars, dried fruit, or trail mix will allow you to stave off drops in your blood-sugar level, which can be not only annoying but downright dangerous.

Fitness & Safety

Physical Preparedness: To complete the rides contained in this book, you should be in at least moderately good physical shape—able to ride 10 or 12 miles with relative ease. While the level-1 rides should not prove terribly taxing, it is still advisable for you to do some cycling prior to your trip if you do not exercise regularly or have not been on a bicycle in some time. The better condition you are in, the more enjoyable the rides will be—and the less likely your body will be prone to injury. Any cardiovascular exercise, including walking and swimming, is good preparation for cycling.

If you have any questions about your physical condition, select the shorter, level-1 rides. Most important, if you have not had a recent physical examination, you should see your doctor.

Prior to your ride, do warm-up leg-stretching exercises for 10 or 15 minutes. You should stretch again after your ride, while your muscles are still warm. Ask at your local bike shop if you are unsure how to stretch properly.

Safety: Remember that the British drive on the left ("opposite") side of the road. British drivers are generally courteous and respectful of cyclists. You need to return the favor and obey all traffic laws, including stopping at stop signs. Ride on the shoulder, with—not against—the flow of traffic. Use hand signals to indicate turns, slowing down, and stopping. Cede right-of-way to walkers and horseback riders on paths, and give adequate warning of your approach by calling out "on your left (or right)" or ringing your bell if you have one. On busy roads and paths, ride in single file, maintaining a distance of at least 10 feet between bicycles.

Carry identification, medical tags if needed, some cash, and a credit card with you on your cycling excursions. And wear light or bright colors and use clothing with reflective strips in dim light.

Taking Your Own Bike—Or Renting One Abroad

Once you've decided to take a vacation that involves cycling in Britain, you face a decision: Should you take your own bicycle (assuming you own one in good working order) or should you rent one abroad? If you cycle frequently, own a decent bicycle, and plan on what might be called a "cycling vacation," I would suggest you take your bike on the plane with you. Have it looked at by a bike mechanic and get a tune-up before leaving on vacation. Spokes, tires, brakes, gear mechanisms, and lubrication should all be checked.

If you plan to bike only a day or two on your trip, you'd be better off renting (or "hiring") a bicycle locally. The ride descriptions in this book list bike shops where you should have no trouble doing this. You can also check out some of the Web sites listed below; they will also point you to rental shops. The **Cyclists' Touring Club** maintains a comprehensive listing of cycle hire outlets around Britain. You may want to call before you leave home and reserve a bike.

If you plan to purchase a bicycle for your trip, do so at a reputable specialist dealer. Proper sizing and explanation of gear shifting is essential,

and salespeople at many department stores are not trained to perform these tasks adequately.

Transporting Your Bike By Plane: For overseas travel to Britain from the U.S., the following airlines allow a bicycle as one checked piece of luggage: **British Air, Virgin, American, Continental,** and **TWA.** (*Note:* Virgin allows only one piece of checked baggage in economy class.) **Delta** charges $75 for a standard, boxed bicycle, independent of the number of checked pieces, while **United** charges an additional $60 for a bike.

Transit requires boxing up your bicycle in a standard cardboard bike box (ask for one at your local bike store; they're always throwing them out) or in a hard or soft carrying case. You'll need to remove the pedals and rotate the handlebars. Carry the necessary tools to reassemble your bicycle once you land.

By Boat: Most ferries and hovercraft serving England from the Continent allow passengers to carry their bicycles free of charge. Check in advance to see if reservations are necessary,

Renting a bike in Britain is simple

and be sure to lock your bike even if you leave it in a special storage area.

By Channel Tunnel: You are allowed to travel with your bicycle on either **Le Shuttle** (☎ 011-44/1303-273-300 or 011-44/990-353535) or **Eurostar** (☎ 800/EUROSTAR or ☎ 011-44/990-300-003), but advance booking is required. To travel on Le Shuttle with a bike, call the 273-300 number at least three days in advance. Cyclists are picked up at the Eurotunnel Customer Service Center (in Britain) and driven to Le Shuttle. Pick-ups occur twice a day if they've been scheduled. The cost is £15 one-way or round-trip. You must pay the driver in cash. To bring a bike on the Eurostar you must disassemble it and place it in a bike bag or box. It is considered luggage, so there is no fee and reservations aren't necessary.

By Train: Most British trains have limited capacity for bicycles. Count on making advance reservations—as far in advance as possible. Some trains will not allow bikes during peak commuter hours. For a fee of £3, you can take your bike to any destination in the U.K. Rail service in Britain is regional, so travelers must check with the appropriate regional railway service. You can reach **BritRail** in the U.S. at ☎ 800/677-8585, but there seems to be some confusion about actual bike policies in Britain. Apparently travelers frequently are able to board along with their bikes without paying a fee; if you are assessed a supplemental charge, however, it should be £3. Check at the ticket window before you board.

European Bike Express: This unique luxury coach and cycle trailer service for cyclists allows you to transport your bike from a number of European destinations straight to Britain. Contact the organization at 31 Baker Street, Middlesbrough, Cleveland TS1 2LF, England [☎(011-44-1642) 251-440 or ☎ (011-44-1642) 750-077; fax (011-44-1642) 232-209].

For further information on bicycle transport, contact the **Cyclists' Touring Club** (CTC) via their Web site, below.

Informational Web Sites

Cruise the Internet before you begin to pedal for additional information on lodging, routes, maps, rentals, and tours:

www.cycling.uk.com This Web site, maintained by the British Department of Transport, lists bike rental centers in Britain by region and contains information on transporting bicycles.

www.ctc.org.uk Cyclists' Touring Club (CTC), Britain's largest cycling organization, operates this site. It offers cycling links and information on touring clubs, newsgroups, events, routes and services, as well as a comprehensive listing of bike rental outlets throughout Britain.

www.visitbritain.com British Tourism's home page contains all matter of concerns facing the bicycle tourist: lodging, maps, bike rental shops, road rules, routes, and special offers. Click on the "Britain for Cyclists" page.

www.holiday.scotland At this site you'll find information on cycling tours, routes, rentals and lodging throughout Scotland.

—Neil E. Schlecht

Wadebridge and The Camel Trail

RIDE 1
CORNWALL
SW989725

INFORMATION

Total Distance
24 miles (38.5km), with 11 miles
(17.5km) off-road

Grade
2

OS Map
Landranger 1:50,000 sheet 200
(Newquay & Bodmin)

Tourist Information
Wadebridge, tel: 01208 813725

Nearest Railway Station
Bodmin Parkway

This ride, travelling mostly along country lanes, takes you through the undulating countryside and unspoiled villages between the north Cornish coast and the imposing flanks of Bodmin Moor. The route includes a delightfully level cycle along an 11-mile (17.5km) section of the picturesque old Bodmin to Wadebridge railway – The Camel Trail. (The ride can be extended along the Camel Trail to explore the estuary and the resort town of Padstow.)

Cycle Shop/Hire
Bridge Bike Hire, Wadebridge,
tel: 01208 813050; Cycle Revolution,
tel: 01208 812021

Refreshments
Pubs and cafés in Wadebridge, and
pubs at St Kew Highway,
St Mabyn and in Dunmere.
The Maltsters Arms at Chapel Amble
has a family room,
and The
St Kew Inn at St Kew a
pleasant garden

*The section of the route along
The Camel Trail offers ideal
conditions for cycling on the level*

START & ROUTE DIRECTIONS

Start

Wadebridge is a small town on the A39 between Bude and Truro, 7 miles (11.5km) north-west of Bodmin. There is a car park on the link road between West Hill and Eddystone Road.

Directions

1 🚲 Turn right out of the car park, then right again at the roundabout into Eddystone Road. On reaching the crossroads in the town centre, turn left and cross the medieval bridge over the River Camel, soon to bear left along the former A39. After nearly ½ mile (1km) turn left on to the B3314, signposted to Rock. Proceed for 1 mile (1.5km) and cross the River Amble (traffic lights), with good views of the Camel estuary and Padstow. In a further mile go over Gutt Bridge and turn immediately right to join a minor road, signed to Chapel Amble.

2 🚲 Continue for 1½ miles (2.5km) to a T-junction in Chapel Amble. Turn right, then left beyond The Maltsters Arms, and follow an undulating road to a crossroads. Keep straight on, then shortly bear right for St Kew. In ¼ mile (0.5km) turn left, then almost immediately right, soon to bear right again, downhill into the picturesque village of St Kew. Pass the inn, climb round a sharp bend, then take the second lane left, signed to St Kew Highway and Donkey Sanctuary. Keep right at a T-junction and shortly enter St Kew Highway, bearing right at The Red Lion to reach the A39.

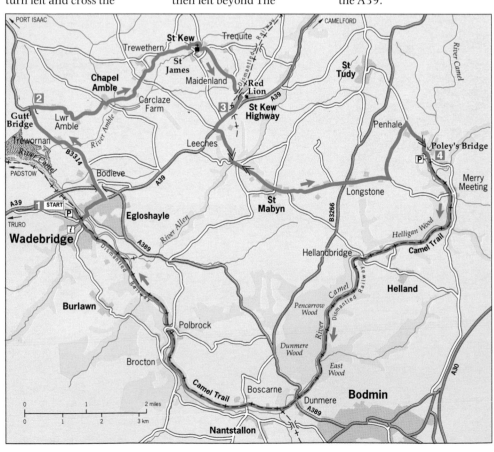

③ ۶s Taking great care, turn right and continue along this busy road for ½ mile (1km), to take the first turning left, signed 'St Mabyn'. Steeply descend (beware of sharp left-hand bend), cross the River Allen and climb steadily (you may need to walk your bike initially) to St Mabyn. Go straight through the village and in 1½ miles (2.5km) reach the Longstone crossroads at the B3266. Continue straight across, then in 1 mile (1.5km) turn left and proceed to a T-junction in 1½ miles (2.5km),

turning right downhill to Poley's Bridge. Cross the bridge and bear right at a car park to join The Camel Trail.

④ ۶s Remain on this level former railway track as it winds its way through woods and open fields beside the fast-flowing River Camel. The surface is very good, but as there are several locked gates along the route, you will have to dismount and wheel your bike around steel barriers. *Note:* be extra careful when crossing the A389 at

Dunmere Bridge, the traffic is fast on the steep hills either side; you are advised to dismount and cross on foot. Also, remember that the Trail is popular with walkers. Follow the Trail for 11 miles (17.5km) back into Wadebridge, meeting traffic at Southern Way. Proceed along The Platt (cycle lane), then at the crossroads in the town centre, go straight on into Eddystone Road, and return to the car park.

On the shore, near the old quarries

PLACES OF INTEREST

Wadebridge: The centrepiece of this small market town at the head of the Camel estuary is the fine medieval bridge spanning the river to Egloshayle. Built by Thomas Lovibond in about 1468, but widened since, it is the longest bridge in Cornwall at 320ft (98m) and originally had 17 arches. It is known as 'The Bridge on Wool', for the pillars are believed to have been built on packs of wool laid down as a foundation to hold the shifting sand of the river. Wadebridge was once a busy port importing coal, timber and limestone, while exporting iron ore and china clay.

St Kew: This delightful little village stands in an idyllic streamside setting. It comprises a 15th-century stone-built inn, an elegant Georgian vicarage, a few houses and a splendid 15th-century church. Some of the finest medieval glass in Cornwall can be seen in St James's Church, one window depicting Christ's Passion and the other with fragments from the Tree of Jesse. The garden of The St Kew Inn is an excellent spot to absorb the peace and quiet of this tucked-away place.

Camel Trail: This attractive recreational walking and cycling route follows the old Bodmin to Wadebridge railway line. Opened in 1834, one of the world's very first steam railways,

The boatyard, Wadebridge

it was originally built to bring in sea sand from the Camel estuary to sweeten the acidic soils on farms inland. In return, granite and china clay were shipped out of Wadebridge. The railway later carried passengers and became a popular way for holidaymakers to travel to Padstow. It closed in 1967, but it was not until 1980 that Cornwall County Council bought a section of the route and converted it into a leisure amenity.

WHAT TO LOOK OUT FOR

The dense woodland and river meadows of the Camel Valley provide a rich habitat for a diverse variety of wildlife, which is best appreciated from a relaxed cycle along the peaceful Camel Trail. The river itself supports salmon, dipper and kingfisher, and on the estuary curlew and shelduck are commonly seen. Resident mammals include fox, badger, rabbit and deer, and you may spot the signs of otters. A wealth of flora includes foxglove, mullein and campion.

RIDE 2
DEVON
SS555325

The Tarka Trail

The Tarka Trail is a 180 mile (290km) long footpath which explores the area described by Henry Williamson in his 1927 nature tale, Tarka the Otter; the lovely southern part of the trail, included here, runs along a former railway track. This ride goes from Barnstaple to Bideford, with the option to extend it as far as Old Torrington Station. It is flat, and provides safe, easy cycling for families.

INFORMATION

Total Distance
18 miles (29km);
with optional extension to
29 miles (46.5km)

Grade
1

OS Map
Landranger 1:50,000 sheet 180
(Barnstaple & Ilfracombe)

Tourist Information
Barnstaple, tel: 01271 388583

Cycle Shops/Hire
Tarka Trail Cycle Hire, Railway Station,
Barnstaple, tel: 01271 24202;
Bideford Bicycle Hire, Bideford,
tel: 01237 424123

Nearest Railway Station
Barnstaple

Refreshments
Pubs and cafés in Barnstaple and
Bideford; The Puffing Billy pub at old
Torrington Station welcomes families

The Tarka Trail by the river at Fremington Quay

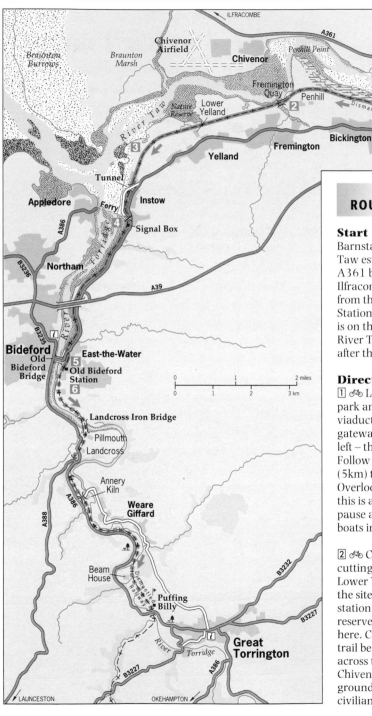

START & ROUTE DIRECTIONS

Start

Barnstaple is at the end of the Taw estuary, and lies on the A361 between Tiverton and Ilfracombe. Begin the ride from the Barnstaple Railway Station car parking area. This is on the south side of the River Taw, just off the B3233 after the river bridge.

Directions

1️⃣ 🚲 Leave the station car park and go under the B3233 viaduct, to pass through a gateway on to a track on your left – this is the Tarka Trail. Follow this track for 3 miles (5km) to Fremington Quay. Overlooking the River Taw, this is a pleasant place to pause and admire the many boats in the creek.

2️⃣ 🚲 Continue through a cutting, and go straight on to Lower Yelland, where there is the site of an old power station. There is a nature reserve in the marshy bay here. Continue and where the trail begins to bear left, look across the Taw to see Chivenor Airfield, a landing ground with a long history of civilian and military flying.

3 🚲 Follow the trail towards Instow, with good views of the open sea towards Lundy Island and Appledore on the opposite side of the River Torridge. Just before Instow, the track passes through a lit tunnel, to arrive at the level-crossing gates. There is still a signal box at this junction; it is looked after by local enthusiasts (who would dearly like to reinstate the railway line), and is sometimes open to view. (In summer you can catch the ferry from Instow Quay across to Appledore and back.)

4 🚲 Leave Instow and follow the track southwards beside the River Torridge. On the opposite bank is Northam. Pass under the A39 to reach a settlement with the quaint name of East-the-Water; beyond this, for contrast, is the old Bideford bridge with its many arches.

5 🚲 Reach the site of the old Bideford station, where snacks and souvenirs are sold from an old railway carriage. Just across the bridge is the town of Bideford, and its many attractions could make it the end of your ride south. Retrace the outward journey to return to the start.

6 🚲 To extend the ride, you can continue on the Tarka Trail for another 5 miles (8km) or so of attractive

The spire of St Peter's Church in Barnstaple bears the date 1636

scenery and woodland: cross the Land Cross iron bridge, go through a tunnel, and cross three more bridges before reaching the Old Station at Great Torrington (now a cheerful pub).

Don't miss Barnstaple's famous pannier market

PLACES OF INTEREST

Barnstaple: The busy centre for north Devon, Barnstaple is one of the oldest boroughs in the country. A magnificent 16-arch bridge, dating from the 16th century, spans the River Taw here, just before it broadens into the estuary. The castle mound, opposite the Civic Centre, is an indication of the fortifications which once surrounded the town. Don't miss the vast, covered Pannier

Sand dunes at Braunton Burrows

Market, and look out for the oddly twisted spire of St Peter's, the parish church, apparently struck by lightning in 1810.

Chivenor Airfield: In 1940 the small grass aerodrome here was developed into a modern airfield with permanent buildings, hangars and runways. With its proximity to the coast, it was used extensively by Coastal Command of the Royal Air Force in their work in the Western Approaches during World War II. An unexpected gift from the enemy came in the form of a Junkers Ju 88A 5 aircraft which landed at Chivenor, mistaking the base for one in France. As a result of recent cutbacks, the station is to close, and be left on a care and maintenance basis. Only the Air-Sea Rescue helicopters of 22 Squadron will remain.

Appledore: This picturesque village near the mouth of the estuary, affectionately described by Charles Kingsley in his locally-set novel *Westward Ho!* (1855), is a popular centre for holidaymakers. The North Devon Maritime Museum tells the history of the village and its strong links with ship-building over the centuries (opening times vary, tel: 01237 474852 for information).

WHAT TO LOOK OUT FOR

The Tarka Trail celebrates the story of an otter, but don't expect to see one – otters are very shy creatures, and while they do still live on the rivers and streams of Devon, you will be lucky to see more than footprints in the mud. However, there is plenty of other wildlife to look out for, especially wading birds, such as oystercatchers, curlew, dunlin, ringed plover and avocet who flock to the rich mudflats of the Taw estuary. Across the estuary, the sand dunes of Braunton Burrows are a nature reserve.

A Round Trip from Exminster to Dawlish

This ride takes you through fine Devon countryside and along the River Exe. It uses, in the main, quiet undulating lanes with no off-road cycling, but for a busier scene, there are opportunities to stop at the seaside resorts of Dawlish Warren and Dawlish.

RIDE 3
DEVON
SX945875

INFORMATION

Total Distance
18 miles (29km)

Grade
2

OS Map
Landranger 1:50,000
sheet 192
(Exeter & Sidmouth)

Tourist Information
Exeter, tel: 01392 265700

Cycle Shops/Hire
Richard's Bikes, Exeter,
tel: 01392 79688;
Saddles and Paddles, Exeter,
tel: 01392 424241

Nearest Railway Station
Exeter St Davids
(2½ miles/4km)

Refreshments
Pubs in Exminster include
The Stowey Arms, and
The Turf by the river;
also Drons Lodge at
Dawlish Warren,
and Bow Windows at Dawlish

The floral gardens beside the river at Dawlish are a great attraction

START & ROUTE DIRECTIONS

Start

Exminster is just off the Matford roundabout on the A379, south of the city of Exeter, and not far from junction 30 of the M5. The ride starts from the car parking area in the centre of the town,

where there are a public telephone box and toilets.

Directions

1️⃣ 🚲 Turn left from the car park to head down to Exminster Hill, where a right turn by Exminster Chapel brings the first steep hill. Continue to the top and, ignoring the right turn to

Soloman Farm, carry straight on down past Crablake Farm, for 1 mile (1.5km) to reach the junction with the A379. Cross the A379 with care to Red Lodge, signposted 'Powderham'. Down this road, to your left, there are good views of a round house, the river and the ship canal. Topsham and Exton can be seen across the river. Continue straight on towards Powderham. Pass the Castle Tower on your right, and follow the road past the gates of Powderham Castle Estate. Bear left towards St Clement's Church at the bottom of the avenue of trees and follow the road sharp right around the church.

2️⃣ 🚲 Continue on this road between the railway and the estate, where you may catch a glimpse of the deer herd. Pass the Starcross Sailing Club on the left, with good views of Lympstone and Exmouth across the river, and reach a junction with the A379. Bear left here, towards Starcross. Just past the public toilets, look out for a red sandstone tower on the left of the road: this is Brunel's Pumping House. Stay on the A379 to Cockwood Harbour, and turn left towards Dawlish Warren.

3️⃣ 🚲 Ignore right turns and proceed along the riverside to a T-junction, just past Dawlish Sands Holiday Camp. Turn right to pass Drons Lodge, and go up a short, steep rise. Continue, past The Mount Pleasant Inn and the Langstone Cliff Hotel, towards Dawlish, to turn left at the

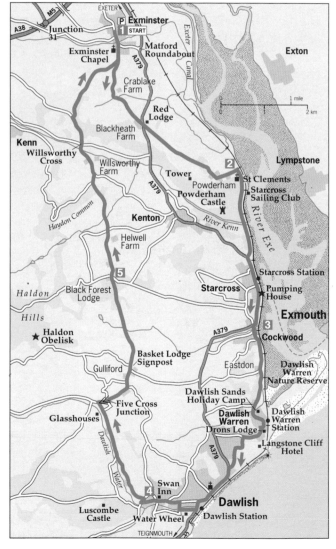

T-junction, back on to the A379. Cycling parallel to the sea front, enter a traffic calming area. Pass a church on the right and on descending a hill, bear left, following the road to the sea front. Keep on this road around a stream area, and bear right and left to go up-stream. Pass a large water-wheel on the left and proceed to the T-junction, at end of Brunswick Place. Turn right and bear right, to turn left up Queen Street. Follow the road around to the left on Park Road, passing the RAFA and British Legion Clubs on the right. Continue into Old Town Street, and on to narrow blind corner. Turn right with care, passing The Swan Inn, and bear left towards Ashcombe.

4 🚲 At a T-junction turn right up an extremely steep but short hill and bear left to follow beside Dawlish Water

Thatched cottages at Powderham

for nearly 2 miles (3km). Ignore the right turn by nursery greenhouses, but take the next right, signposted to Starcross, up narrow rise. At the top, to the left is a view of the Haldon Obelisk. Descend with care, heading straight across a five-point junction, down long hill. Bear

left at the bottom to pass Gulliford House and reach the 'Basket Lodge' signpost. Continue straight on, signposted 'Starcross'. Ignore all turnings until the Black Forest Lodge is reached, after about 1½ miles (2.5km).

5 🚲 Cross straight over this junction, but take great care, as the left side is blind. Proceed straight on, crossing Haydon Common, past Willsworthy Farm, and on to Willsworthy Cross crossroads. At this junction proceed straight ahead up the hill and at the next junction, turn right towards Exminster. Follow this lane to a T-junction. Turn left here, down a steep hill into the village; turn left at the T-junction at the bottom of the hill, and retrace your route to the car park.

Powderham Castle

PLACES OF INTEREST

Exminster: Set on the west bank of the River Exe, Exminster has become a peaceful, pleasant backwater of a town since the building of a by-pass. The church dates back as far as the 8th century and has a notable set of bells.

Powderham Castle: The home of the Earl of Devon is a medieval fortified manor house, extended and altered in the 18th and 19th centuries, but with a core some 400 years older, and commands wonderful views over the estate to the river. Flamboyantly decorated rooms are beautifully furnished, and the castle is well worth a

visit (open from the end of March to early October). The extensive grounds are home to a large herd of fallow deer, and these can often be glimpsed from the road to Starcross through Powderham.

Starcross: Isambard Kingdom Brunel, the great Victorian engineer, had much to do with the development of the south-west, thanks to his involvement in the Great Western Railway system. The strange red-brick Pumping Tower in Starcross is about all that remains of his experimental 'atmospheric railway', by which trains were running at up to 70mph as

Brunel's Pumping Station

early as 1818. During the summer months, a ferry plies between Starcross and Exmouth.

Dawlish: This quaint holiday town is a pleasant place to explore, with the Dawlish Water stream running through the centre. This provides a haven of peace with a lovely miniature garden complete with cascading waterfalls, many ducks, and the famous Dawlish black swans being fed by the visitors. Artist Alwyn Crawshaw's studio stands on the heights above the town centre, and it is easy to understand the appeal of this lovely location. The railway which runs along the coast here is one of the prettiest routes in England. The sand dunes of nearby Dawlish Warren provide a haven for birdlife, and golfers. It is worth walking along to the prominent Langstone Rock area for views up and down the coast. *Note:* cycling along the sea-wall is prohibited.

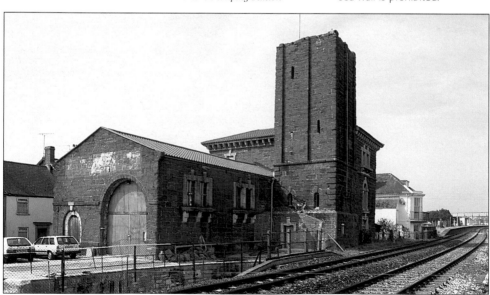

Bulbarrow and Milton Abbas

RIDE 4
DORSET
ST784059

This is a fairly demanding but thoroughly enjoyable ride in the very scenic and often windswept heart of Dorset. The route is mostly along peaceful undulating lanes, with the occasional green lane and stone track.

INFORMATION

Total Distance
11 miles (17.5km),
with 3 miles (5km) off-road

Grade
3

OS Map
Landranger 1:50,000 sheet 194
(Dorchester & Weymouth)

Tourist Information
Blandford, tel: 01258 454770

Nearest Railway Station
Sherborne/Dorchester
(12 miles/19.5km)

Refreshments
Tea room at Park Farm;
pub and tea rooms in Milton Abbas;
The Fox Inn in Lower Ansty has good
facilities for children

The view from Bulbarrow viewpoint is superb

START & ROUTE DIRECTIONS

Start

The route starts from the viewpoint high on Bulbarrow Hill, west of Blandford Forum, where there is a broad layby in which to park. To reach it turn off the A354 Blandford to Puddletown road at Winterborne Whitechurch and follow the signs to Bulbarrow.

Directions

1️⃣ 🚴 From the car park turn left and left again, heading south-east. Fork left at the junction, signposted to Turnworth and Winterborne Stickland, and cycle on to shortly reach a signed bridleway on the right.

(During very wet weather an alternative route is to carry on down the lane keeping right to Winterborne Houghton, and turn right again in the village centre to meet up with the main route at 2️⃣ below).

Dismount and push your bike across the verge and through the small farm gate. Bearing left, cycle half-way across the field then arc left down the hillside to the gate. Pass through onto the flint track (stony in places) and coast down through attractive bluebell woods to a second gate, leading to Heath Bottom. The grass track gently descends through the

The distinctive broad main street of Milton Abbas, a model village

valley before reaching another farm gate. Continue past the dwellings, and down the metalled lane through Higher Houghton to the valley. Turn right on to the bridleway, signposted 'Milton Abbas'.

2️⃣ 🚴 The wide, slightly uneven stone track, home to hartstongue ferns and primroses, rises quite steeply to a gate – all but the fittest will need to dismount and walk for at least part of the way.

Bear left up the grassy hillside to the gate at the top, taking time to look back and enjoy the view. Turn onto a grass track, following it up to the gate. Turn right into the lane.

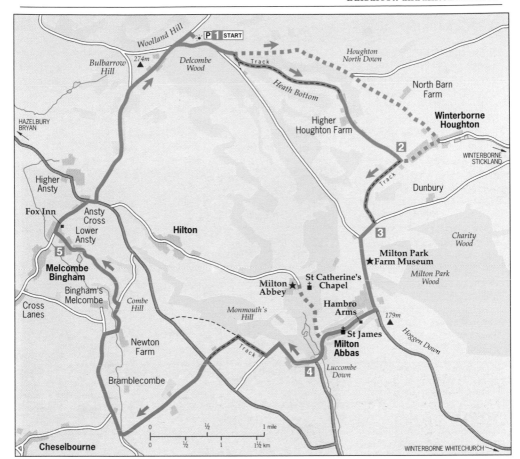

3 🚲 After a short distance, bear left at the junction. A short stretch of level road precedes a gradual descent towards Milton Abbas, passing Milton Park Farm Museum on the left. Turn right at the sign for Milton Abbas, continue past The Hambro Arms and through the delightful thatched village. Turn right at the bottom to visit the Abbey, or left to continue the main cycle route.
Pass the lake and take the turning on the right, signed to Lower Ansty Cross and Hazelbury Bryan.

4 🚲 The road rises steadily beside an old flint stone wall and woods on the left filled with wild ramsons in early spring. Pedal up and round a sharp left-hand bend, looking out for a grassy track on the right between two field gates. Cycle up this green lane to the top and turn left. The grass gives way to a gravel surface before reaching the road. Cross into the lane opposite, signposted 'Cheselbourne'. After a long and enjoyable descent, cross the bridge and turn right at a T-junction towards Melcombe Bingham. After cycling gently downhill, turn right before Bingham's Melcombe, cross the bridge and turn left, following an attractive winding lane through to Lower Ansty.

5 🚲 In Lower Ansty, turn right. (The Fox Inn is an ideal refreshment stop, and even provides a hot shower for the convenience of cyclists.) Continue past the pub, to turn right at the T-junction. Shortly, take the next turning left, signed 'Bulbarrow'. After about a mile fork right, and go right again at the top of the hill to return to the car park.

PLACES OF INTEREST

Milton Park Farm Museum:
Open from Easter, this fascinating museum, housed in a thatched former carthorse stables, has an extensive collection of rural and domestic bygones built up over four generations by the Fookes family who still live here. Outside you can see the Reverend Fletcher's unique collection of chimney pots and select herbs from the herb train. Children can amuse themselves in the play area or feed and touch all the animals – which include pigs, calves, horses, donkeys, goats, Jacob sheep, bantams and ducks.

Milton Abbas: This curious village of largely uniform houses, set on broad strips of green lawn to either side of the main street, was built in the 1770s by Joseph Damer, Earl of Dorchester. He had built a magnificent house next to the old abbey, and regarded the existing old market town as an eyesore. After demolishing all the old houses (despite fierce local opposition), he built the present model village. Most of the cob cottages are thatched and painted white. In the centre of the village stand some 17th-century brick-and-flint almshouses and the 18th-century church of St James, which was designed in late Georgian style to blend in with the village.

Milton Abbey: Joseph Damer's huge gothic mansion, now a school, is on the site of an abbey founded in AD938 by King Athelstan. Apart from the Abbot's Hall, nothing remains of the older buildings except the fine abbey church. Inside, the superb carved oak shrine, in which the consecrated host was kept, is unique, for no others escaped destruction during the Reformation. In the grounds of Milton Abbey there is an unusual staircase consisting of 111 turf steps leading up to a 12th-century chapel dedicated to St Catherine. According to legend it was built on the spot where King Athelstan camped on his way to battle, having had a vision ensuring his victory.

The fine abbey church at Milton Abbas

The Bristol and Bath Cycleway

RIDE 5
AVON
ST738653

INFORMATION

Total Distance
21 miles (33.5km)

Grade
2

OS Map
Landranger 1:50,000 sheet 172
(Bristol & Bath)

Tourist Information
Bath, tel: 01225 462831; Bristol,
tel: 01179 260767

Starting in the historic spa-town of Bath, this route makes use of the famous Bristol and Bath Cycle Path. Constructed by the Bristol-based charity Sustrans, this was the first major urban cycle/pedestrian route in the country. The ride loops down through Keynsham and pretty villages, to return on the cycleway.

Cycle Shops/Hire
Avon Valley Cyclery (repairs/hire),
Bath, tel: 01225 442442; John's Bikes,
Bath, tel: 01225 334633; Woods
Cycles, Hanham, tel: 01179 352042;
Buggies and Bikes (repairs/hire),
Keynsham, tel: 01179 868184

Nearest Railway Station
Bath

Refreshments
Bath has many pubs, cafés and
restaurants; Avon Valley Railway;
Keynsham has various pubs
and tea rooms;
also good food at The Compton pub,
Compton Dando, where there are
facilities for children

The route starts at the Royal Crescent in the heart of Bath

START & ROUTE DIRECTIONS

Start

Bath is situated on the A4, south-east of Bristol. The route starts at the Victoria Park play area, near Royal Crescent, where there is usually plenty of on-street parking.

Directions

1 潯 Head west from Victoria Park along the A4, towards Bristol. Go straight through the traffic lights by the Fina petrol station, and after a short distance bear left into Locksbrook Road, signposted to the Bristol and Bath Railway Path. Follow this road through the industrial estate, across a mini roundabout, and past The Dolphin pub. A few yards further on reach the canal, and look out for a lock, a short way ahead on the left. As Johnson's newsagency comes into view, take the road on the left and turn immediately right on to the Bristol and Bath Cycle Path.

2 潯 You are now in a traffic-free zone, and can enjoy a lazy, level ride all the way to the Avon Valley Railway some 5 miles (8km) further on. As a general rule, it is best to keep to the left. At intervals along the Cycle Path, notice boards give information about wildlife. There are also rest points. At the Avon Valley Railway there are refreshment facilities, parking and toilets,

Enjoy the Georgian elegance of Pulteney Bridge, Bath

as well as much railway memorabilia to be seen.

3 潯 Leave the railway, and head down the drive to the main road, to turn sharp right under the old railway bridge. At the roundabout, to visit Willsbridge Mill, bear right here, speed down a dip and up the other side. About half way up the rise there is a footpath off to the right which takes you straight into Willsbridge Mill. To rejoin the main route, leave the Mill and turn left down the hill, back to the roundabout. Bear right on to the A4175, signposted 'Keynsham', but take care – this road carries some very heavy traffic. Pedal across the valley floor, passing the Cadbury factory on the right and the Portavon Marina, before

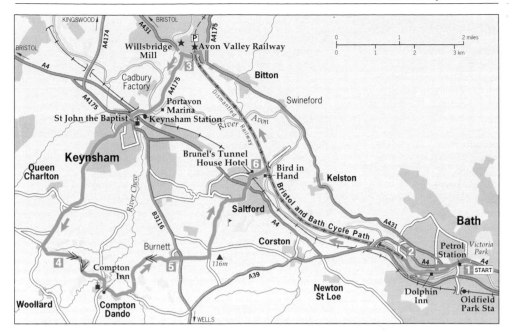

crossing the River Avon. Pedal up the rise past the railway station, and continue to the roundabout by the church of St John the Baptist. Turn left here, and first right into Charlton Road, signposted to Queen Charlton and Whitchurch. Follow the road out into open countryside, forking left to Woollard after 2 miles (3km). Turn left at the unmarked crossroads (with a bungalow on the opposite corner) into a small lane, taking care round the sharp bends at Wooscombe Bottom. Enjoy the views across the open country below and around you. There is a small car park if you need a breather.

4 武 Continue towards Compton Dando – enjoy the descent, but do take care: gravel and a number of sharp corners must be negotiated before you finally drop down into Compton Dando. Turn right out of Peppershells Lane into the village, going over the small, hump-backed bridge. A little further on is The Compton Inn, and the village church is also worth exploring. After crossing the bridge take the first turning left signposted to Burnett and Stanton Prior. Climb up Bathford Hill, away from the village, past the green into open countryside. After ½ mile (1km) take the left fork, dropping into the valley, and continue round the sharp bends at the bottom. Climb up the narrow lane, and up the sharp rise into Burnett.

5 武 Continue to the crossroads and cross straight over the B3116 with great care, into Middlepiece Lane. Continue to a T-junction and turn left. In a short distance, go straight over the crossroads, towards Saltford. Enjoy the freewheel down the side of the wood, passing Lower Fields, and eventually turn right into Manor Road. At the end, turn right again, following the road round the residential area and down to the main road. Take care crossing (use the pelican crossing lights if necessary), and head left, straight down Beech Road. At the bottom turn right into the High Street, opposite Brunel's Tunnel House Hotel, and continue to The Bird in Hand pub. Go down the side of the pub and just under the railway bridge turn right, which leads back on to the cycle path.

6 武 Turn towards Bath, and retrace your route to the start at Victoria Park.

PLACES OF INTEREST

Bath: This lovely city has a wealth of architectural and historical heritage, and it is impossible to see everything. The Baths and the gorgeous, glittering Assembly Rooms are a must on any itinerary though, and there are a number of pleasant green parks dotted round the city. It is a treat just to walk around the town centre, with its elegant shops, and fine architecture.

Much of Bath dates from Georgian times, when Beau Nash and others made it the fashionable town to be seen in. Royal Crescent is a splendid example, and you can visit the first house in the row, No 1, for a glimpse of Georgian elegance and style (open March to December, not Mondays). Other museums to see here include the extraordinary Bath Industrial

Wild flowers bloom in the woodland at Willsbridge Mill

Heritage museum and the prestigious Museum of Costume. If it all seems too busy, take a stroll down by the canal which winds peacefully through the city centre.

Willsbridge Mill: Willsbridge Mill, headquarters of the Avon Wildlife Trust, is a nature oasis just within the bounds of Bristol, and its buildings house many exhibitions and teaching facilities. It is a favourite destination for school parties, but these seldom occur at weekends. There are also many nature trails and 'outdoor experiments' which you can see in operation for yourself.

Two Quiet Villages: Burnett, on the outskirts of Keynsham,

has in its small area a wealth of old buildings which have been carefully looked after. Although one or two sport modern appendages, most retain the original exterior and roof. The village plan has remained unchanged for most of this century, even through the two World Wars, when a local military base (now disused) was established near by. Compton Dando sits in the bottom of the valley, bisected by the River Chew. The church is sited some little way off the village centre, but the walk up Church Lane can bring a welcome relief from sitting in the saddle. The village dates back to medieval times, and the overall effect is peaceful and tranquil.

WHAT TO LOOK OUT FOR

The northern section of the disused railway line on this route, the Avon Walkway, passes through the Avon Valley Country Park.

Marlborough and the Kennet and Avon Canal

The route begins at Marlborough and takes in a number of small picturesque villages and wooded valleys. It also follows part of the peaceful Kennet and Avon Canal, passing several interesting places to visit. The cycling is relatively easy for the most part, but there are two short, steep climbs and two fast, steep descents where particular care will be needed; beware of mud or loose gravel on the lanes.

RIDE 6
WILTSHIRE
SU187690

INFORMATION

Total Distance
26 miles (41.5km)

Grade
2

OS Map
Landranger 1:50,000 sheets 173
(Swindon & Devizes) and 174
(Newbury & Wantage)

Tourist Information
Marlborough, tel: 01672 513989

Cycle Shops/Hire
Cyclecare (repairs), Pewsey,
tel: 01672 564435; Town Mill Cycles
(some hire), Marlborough,
tel: 01672 514914

Nearest Railway Station
Bedwyn; also Pewsey and
Hungerford

Refreshments
Marlborough offers a wide variety of
pubs and cafés, including the excellent
Polly Tea Rooms on the High Street.
Along the route, pubs include The Red
Lion at Axford (good food), and The
Cross Keys in Great Bedwyn, which
welcomes children and has special
secure facilities for cycles.
Good picnic spots beside the canal, or
in Savernake Forest

The ancient trees of Savernake Forest provide plenty of shady picnic spots

START & ROUTE DIRECTIONS

Start
The route starts in the small town of Marlborough, where the A4 and the A436 meet, south of Swindon. Park in the wide main street (free) or in one of the public car parks.

Directions
[1] From the centre of Marlborough head east along the main street towards Hungerford. At the end bear left to pass the Imperial Cancer Research Fund shop, and take the first turn right into Silverless Street. Follow this to the end, and go straight across into St Martins, signed to Mildenhall, Aldbourne and Ramsbury. Follow this minor road through the outskirts of Marlborough, and enjoy a short descent to the river, crossing the bridge at the bottom. The road then rises gently, with good views of the River Kennet to your right. Cross over the disused railway bridge, and follow the road for 1 mile (1.5km) to Mildenhall. Pass The Horseshoes on the left. Follow the road round to the right and continue on this road beside the river towards Ramsbury. Continue past Durnsford Mill and the Granary Kitchen tea rooms, to reach Axford.

[2] Pedal up the rise and through Axford, past the church, and enjoy the views of the river meandering through the meadows below. Stay on this road as it veers away from the river and at the fork, bear right, following signs for Ramsbury. Follow

the undulating road through the wood, looking out for Ramsbury Manor on the right. After a long straight descent, the road bends left into Ramsbury itself.

[3] Follow the High Street to pass a row of houses with a brick-and-flint façade. At the end of the High Street fork right, then take the next right turn, signed 'Froxfield'. Cross the bridge (look out for ducks) to embark on a short but steep climb through the Z-bends. At the next junction turn left, still signed to Froxfield. After 2 undulating miles (3km) the road narrows, leading into Froxfield. Take care on the narrow bends as you reach the village. Continue to meet the main road (A4).

[4] Bear left here, towards Hungerford; pass a long row of alms houses, to turn right after The Pelican pub, signposted to Little Bedwyn. Cross the railway bridge, then the bridge over the canal, then bear right to follow the Kennet and Avon Canal for about 1½ miles (2.5km) to Little Bedwyn. Follow the brick wall round to the left, then turn right for

The extraordinary Stone Museum

Great Bedwyn. Cross over the railway bridge then bear left for Great Bedwyn. Turn left at The Three Tuns as you come into the village, then turn right into Church Street, opposite the Cross Keys.

[5] Continue on Church Street, passing the unusual Stone Museum. Shortly after leaving the village turn right, signposted 'Crofton' (rather than go over the railway bridge), and continue parallel with the railway. Head into Crofton, past the thatched cottages and up the rise, to pass the Crofton Beam Engines. Follow the road over the railway bridge – you're now between the railway and the canal. The road swings over the canal bridge, then bear right towards Wolfhall and Burbage. Climb up through the farmyard complex at Wolfhall and go on to Burbage. Bear right through the out-skirts of the village and turn right on to the main street.

[6] After ½ mile (1km) turn right at The Three Horseshoes at Stibb Green, and follow this road for ¾ mile (1km) past the

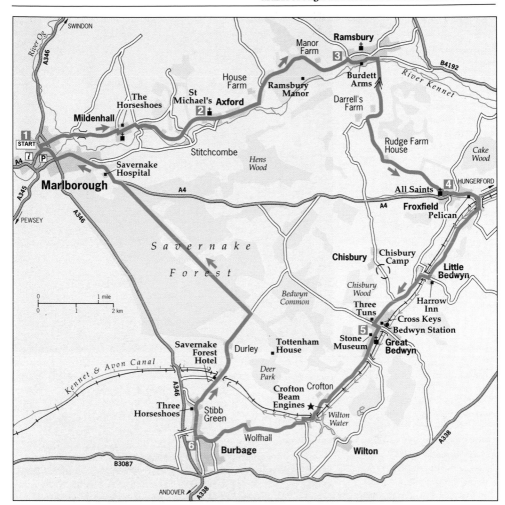

Savernake Forest Hotel, and over the railway line. Start the gentle climb out of the valley, looking across the deer park, right, to see Tottenham House. A short way further on, turn left opposite a brick and ironwork gateway, into Savernake Forest. Follow this road for 3 miles (5km) straight through the forest, passing through the gates at the far end. Turn left on to the

A4 towards Marlborough, passing the Savernake Hospital, and drop down the long, steep descent into

Marlborough. Bear right at the first roundabout, and left at the second, back into the town centre.

The Kennet and Avon Canal

PLACES OF INTEREST

Marlborough: From the lively mix of buildings along Marlborough's broad High Street, you could be forgiven for believing this a Georgian market town. A foray down almost any side street however reveals the wooden timbering of much earlier houses. In fact, much more of the town would have been timbered and thatched, like the surrounding villages, but a series of major fires in the 17th century resulted in a thatching ban. It is a pleasing place, dominated at its western end by the famous public school, Marlborough College, and with lots of interesting old corners to explore.

Froxfield: The almshouses of this little village were the gift in 1694 of Sarah, the dowager Duchess of Somerset, to house poor widows. The story of 'Wild' Darrell is also linked with Froxfield – accused of throwing a new-born baby on to a fire, he was pursued by the Hounds of Hell.

The Kennet and Avon Canal: This scenic waterway was once a main thoroughfare for transporting goods across southern England. Nowadays the boats travel strictly for pleasure, and it is hard to imagine a more relaxing way to see the countryside than from the top of a ponderous long-boat. The canal would have been a life-line to the villages along its length such as Little and Great Bedwyn. Beyond Great Bedwyn, look out for the Crofton Beam Engine, a steam-driven engine which was built

Almshouses chapel, Froxfield

to pump water to the summit level of the canal.

Savernake: Great oaks, elms and beeches dominate this beautiful ancient forest, dating back over 900 years. Once a royal forest, Jane Seymour was the daughter of one of its

wardens, and celebrated her wedding to Henry VIII at nearby Wolfhall. Rare wild flowers grow under the shady canopy of the woods, and forest glades provide ideal picnic spots. The Column, visible through the trees near the south-east end of the Grand Avenue, was raised to mark George III's recovery from madness.

WHAT TO LOOK OUT FOR

Some of the churches along the route contain unexpected delights. The church at Mildenhall, unusually, was completely refitted inside early in the 19th century, and remains a microcosm of that age in oak, including box-pews. A church has stood on the same spot in Ramsbury since Anglo-Saxon times, and fragments of wonderfully carved stone memorials dating from that period may still be seen there today. Look out, too, for the chandeliers in the church – rather more modern, they are 18th-century additions.

RIDE 7
SOMERSET/AVON
ST590526

Chew Valley Lake

Following a leisurely, scenic route around Chew Valley Lake, this ride offers plenty of opportunity to stop and picnic, and to enjoy some wildlife havens. The area can become busy on Bank Holidays and summer weekends.

INFORMATION

Total Distance
19 miles (31km)

Grade
2

OS Map
Landranger 1:50,000 sheet 182
(Weston-super-Mare & Bridgwater)

Tourist Information
Wells, tel: 01749 672552

Cycle Shops/Hire
Wells City Cycles, tel: 01749 675096

Nearest Railway Station
Keynsham

Refreshments
Pubs in both Chew Magna and Chew Stoke; The Kings Arms at Litton; refreshments at Chewton Mendip Cheese Dairy; picnic areas by Chew Valley Lake

Reedbeds on Chew Valley Lake

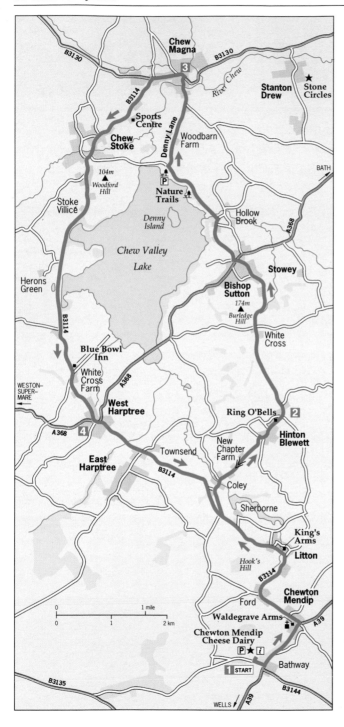

Start
The route starts from the car park of Chewton Mendip Cheese Dairy, which offers refreshments, other attractions and toilets. (The Dairy management request that you park to the far left of the car park as you go in, so if you leave your vehicle all day it does not obstruct other visitors.) The Cheese Dairy is just outside the village, which is on the A39, 5½ miles (9km) north-east of Wells.

Directions
1 ⬚ Cycle up the drive and turn left towards Chewton Mendip. At the T-junction turn left on to the main road (A39) and head down towards the village. Pass The Waldegrave Arms on the left, to turn left at the bottom of the hill on to the B3114, towards West Harptree. Stay on this road to Litton, passing

Cottages in Chewton Mendip, once a centre for lead-mining

The King's Arms on your right. Continue on the B3114 for another mile and take the shallow downhill right turn off the main road (white railings at the junction). Take care following this very narrow lane towards Hinton Blewett. Turn right at the junction just after the bridge over the stream, and climb up to New Chapter Farm. Turn right at the T-junction on the edge of Hinton Blewett, signed 'Bishop Sutton', and follow the road through the village, passing a camping and caravanning site and The Ring o' Bells pub.

2 ⚲ From Hinton Blewett follow signs to Bishop Sutton; go straight over the crossroads and enter the village. At the junction with the main road (A368) go straight across into Ham Lane, signposted to Chew Magna. Follow the lane past The Hollies and out into the country. At the junction bear left on to the main lane, and take the first left, signed to Chew Stoke and Chew Magna. Chew Valley Lake is now on your left. Continue towards Chew Magna, and after ½ mile (1km), reach a picnic site on the left, with toilet facilities. (*Note:* two nature trails run from here: the Bittern Trail and the Grebe Trail, which can be explored at most times of the year.) In ½ mile (1km) pass a second picnic area with facilities, and shortly turn right into Denny Lane, up a short rise. Ahead, Chew Magna comes into view. After 1 mile

The church at Chew Magna

(1.5km) bear left over the hump-backed bridge and into the village centre.

3 ⚲ Bear left through the main street, and turn left on to the B3114 towards Chew Stoke. Follow this road past a sports centre and down into Chew Stoke. Continue on this road through the village, and on towards West Harptree. Again there are wide views over Chew Valley Lake. There is often an ice-cream seller at the lay-by at Herons Green, offering refreshment before the gentle climb back up towards West Harptree. Stay

on the B3114, bearing left just after The Blue Bowl Inn, to pass White Cross Farm, and reach West Harptree.

4 ⚲ Turn left on to the main road (A368), and continue to the end of the High Street. Where the road bears sharp left, turn right on to the B3114, signposted to East Harptree and Chewton Mendip. Follow this road for about 5 miles (8km) back to Chewton Mendip, and retrace your route back to Chewton Mendip Cheese Dairy.

PLACES OF INTEREST

Chewton Mendip: This little grey-stone village on the edge of the rolling Mendip hills has its origins in the local lead-mining industry.
Its clearest landmark is the tall tower of the church, a building with a particularly rich history which dates from Saxon times. The church contains two items of note — a rare 'fryd', or sanctuary stool, and a first edition of the Authorised (King James) Bible, dating from 1611.

Chew Valley Lake: Despite its name and attractive appearance, the lake is actually a man-made reservoir. It has proved a magnet for wildlife and visitors alike, and there are special facilities to enable

WHAT TO LOOK OUT FOR

Chew Valley Lake is an important inland site for wintering wildfowl, including a small but regular flock of Bewick swans. Thousands of tufted duck and gadwall can be seen here between October and March.
The lake is also stocked with brown and rainbow trout, making it popular with anglers.

the latter to make the most of the former! The little island at the northern end is Denny Island.

Chew Magna: This comfortable little town stands just to the north of a fine old bridge across the River Chew. The high street is raised

above the main level, presumably to avoid the dangers of flooding. Don't miss a monument in the church to Sir John Hartville, a very strong man.
On a hill overlooking the town from the north stands Chew Tower, an 18th-century castellated folly.

Detail and gargoyle on the wall of the church, Chew Magna

<table>
<tr><td>RIDE 8
SOMERSET
ST736457</td><td><h1>Nunney and Frome</h1></td></tr>
</table>

Winding between pretty Somerset villages, this route leads through the bustling market town of Frome and back out into rolling countryside, returning via a picturesque moated castle.

INFORMATION

Total Distance
15½ miles (25km)

Grade
2

The picturesque ruin of Nunney Castle

OS Map
Landranger 1:50,000 sheet 183
(Yeovil & Frome)

Tourist Information
Frome, tel: 01373 467271

Cycle Shops/Hire
D J Cycles, Frome, tel: 01373 453563

Nearest Railway Station
Frome

Refreshments
Pubs along the route include
The George at Nunney, The Fox and
Hounds at Tytherington and
The Talbot Inn at Mells; cafés and tea
rooms, as well as Scoffs, in Frome

The ever-popular Cheap Street is one of Frome's finest

START & ROUTE DIRECTIONS

Start

The route starts in the village of Nunney, 3 miles (5km) south-west of Frome, just north of the A361. Park in the village centre car park.

Directions

[1] 搶 From the village centre car park head uphill away from the river, following signs to Witham Friary and Bruton. At the top of the rise turn down the side of The Theobald Arms, following the cycleway signs. Pass under the major road (A361), and

bear left towards Trudoxhill. Go into Trudoxhill, passing The White Hart pub and bear right for Witham and Gare Hill. Just up the following rise, take the right fork for Witham and at the T-junction turn left. Stay on this road, downhill, for about a mile, crossing the River Frome, and eventually running parallel with the railway line. Turn left at the junction signposted to Nunney, and after ¼ mile (0.5km) bear right into a small lane. At the crossroads turn right, pass through the hamlet of Lower Marston, and turn left at the end for Tytherington.

[2] 搶 Pass the site on the left of the former village of Marston, to reach Tytherington. Continue through the village, past The Fox and Hounds, to take the next fork right. Go through a kissing gate, and cycle up the route of the old road. At the far end go through another kissing gate, and cross over the A361 with great care. On the opposite side, take the left fork and climb up the lane. At the end of the lane go straight across into the 'No Through Road', and continue down the side of The Mason's Arms. Continue down this road, squeezing through the bollards at the end, and carry on through the residential area, going straight over each junction to reach Nunney Road. (To take a short-cut straight back to Nunney, turn left here and follow the road down to the car park in the centre of Nunney.) Turn right, and at the T-junction go right again, on to the main A362. At the roundabout turn left, and head down into Frome town centre.

[3] 搶 Cross the river bridge and climb up the hill the other side, taking the second turning left into Welshmill Road. Follow this road into Lower Innox, and climb up through a housing estate. Pass The Farmer's Arms pub, go over the hump-backed bridge, and at the junction turn left. Follow the road under the railway, and climb gently to the A362. Turn right on to the main road, and almost immediately left, signposted to Hapsford and Great Elm. Follow this road

through Great Elm and down into Mells. At the junction at the bottom, bear right and climb up through the village past the war memorial.

4 🚲 Pass the Talbot Inn and take the next turning left, past the Rectory and down a steep hill. Turn right at the bottom and follow the river for a short distance. Where the road continues round to the right, turn left, climbing up from the entrance to Mells Park and past the village school. At the top go straight over the junction, heading for Chantry, and in the village, go straight over the crossroads. The road descends steeply, with a following steep but short climb. Bear left at the top, and continue over the next junction, towards Nunney. At the T-junction bear right, and drop down back into the village centre to return to the car park.

A bird's-eye view of Mells, from the church tower

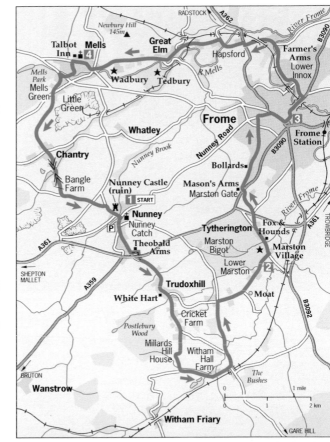

PLACES OF INTEREST

Coppice now grows over part of the site of Tedbury Fort

Nunney Castle: This spectacular ruin is to the north of the village. Originally a narrow rectangle in shape, with great corner towers, some say it was modelled on the Bastille in France. The castle dates back to 1373 and was built by Sir John Delamare, whose tomb is in the village church; he adapted his existing deep-moated manor house, adding crenellations and fortifications. In 1645 the then owner, Sir Richard Prater (whose family are also represented in the church), was besieged in the castle with his followers. The Parliamentarian army succeeded in damaging the castle beyond repair, and it has lain deserted ever since. Houses in the pretty village mostly date to the 1600s or 1700s.

Frome: This busy market town on the River Frome (pronounced 'Froom') is well worth exploring on foot. Of its narrow side-streets the most appealing – and most famous – is Cheap Street, with its steep roofs, timbered buildings and narrow runnel of water down the centre of the road. Don't miss the almshouses near the bridge, which date from the early 18th century, or the parish church, heavily and controversially restored in Victorian times.

Mells: Frequently described as one of Somerset's loveliest villages, Mells combines pretty thatched cottages and pleasing stone houses with a spattering of small greens and a practical, lived-in air. Mells Manor, a Tudor mansion, was the abode of the Horner family. According to legend, the deeds to the manor were hidden in a pie and sent to Henry VIII, but were stolen along the way; this tale is celebrated in the nursery rhyme 'Little Jack Horner'!

WHAT TO LOOK OUT FOR

Along the route there are various signs of much earlier settlements, long deserted. At the junction near Tytherington stood the village of Marston – now the sister villages of Marston Bigot, Marston Gate and Lower Marston are all that survive. On the road to Mells, the earth ramparts of the prehistoric camp at Tedbury are still as high as 15ft (4.5m) in some places; Wadbury Camp, also to the left of this road, is also passed.

A Cotswold Tour from Stow-on-the-Wold

RIDE 9
GLOUCESTERSHIRE
SP191257

This route explores one of the loveliest corners of the Cotswolds, starting from the popular wool town of Stow-on-the-Wold. Look out for mud on the lanes, and don't expect to stay on your bike to the top of every hill!

INFORMATION

Total Distance
24 miles (38.5km)

Grade
3

OS Map
Landranger 1:50,000 sheet 163
(Cheltenham & Cirencester)

Tourist Information
Stow-on-the-Wold, tel: 01451 831082

Cycle Shops/Hire
Hartwells, Bourton-on-the-Water,
tel: 01451 820405;
The Toy Shop, Moreton-in-Marsh,
tel: 01608 650759;
Cotswold Cycle Hire,
tel: 01386 438706

Cottages in Lower Slaughter

Nearest Railway Station
Moreton-in-Marsh (4 miles/6.5km);
Kingham (on route)

Refreshments
Stow and Bourton-on-the-Water have
many cafés and pubs; the
Washbourne Court Hotel at Lower
Slaughter; tea room and The New Inn
at Nether Westcote; Mill House Hotel
at Kingham; The Fox at Broadwell

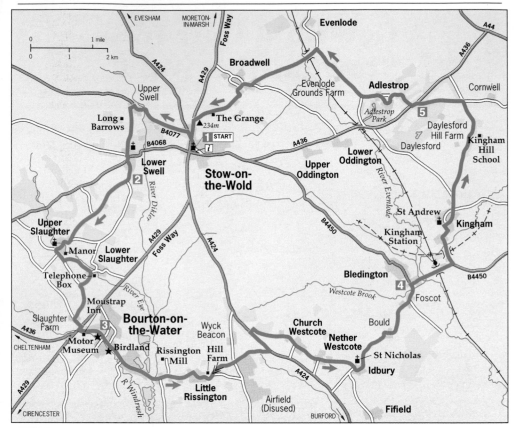

START & ROUTE DIRECTIONS

Start
Stow-on-the-Wold lies between Cheltenham and Banbury, where the A424 crosses the A429. Park with care in the town centre; the ride starts in the town square.

Directions
1 🚲 From the town square head north and follow signs to join the A429 towards Stratford-upon-Avon. After a short distance, turn left at the traffic lights, and left again on to the B4077, signed 'Upper Swell'. The road drops down the hill on a rather rough road surface, with stone walls on both sides and good views. Follow the route over a narrow hump-backed bridge, to climb up into Upper Swell. Turn left on to a small, narrow lane, signposted to Lower Swell and The Slaughters. Pass two ancient long barrows on the right, then drop down past the church into Lower Swell. At the bottom go straight over, keeping the war memorial on your left. Turn right on to the main road by the phone box, then first left, signed 'The Slaughters'. Beyond the village, fork right towards Upper Slaughter.

2 🚲 Drop down into Upper Slaughter, and take the sharp right-hand bend with caution. Follow the road round to the left. Turn right down here to explore the village; otherwise, keep straight on up the rise, heading away from the river, to turn left at the T-junction. Following signs for Lower Slaughter, bear left after ½ mile (1km). Enter Lower Slaughter, parallel with the river, and turn right immediately past the phone box. (To explore the village keep straight on here.) The road rises gently; at the top turn left, signed 'Bourton-on-the-Water'. You can see the

village on the left as you come down the hill. Turn left at the junction, and after a short distance reach the Foss Way (A429). Turn right on to the A429, then left into Lansdown, following the river past The Mousetrap Inn and into Bourton-on-the-Water.

3 ♻ Head straight along the main street; at the end, bear right into Rissington Road. Pass Birdland, and the road starts to climb towards Little Rissington. Pass Rissington Mill on the left, to climb up through the village, and past Hill Farm reach a crossroads (good views back over Little Rissington and Bourton-on-the-Water). At the crossroads go straight over, signposted to Burford, and continue, with Wyck Beacon on your left, to meet the A424. Turn left, towards Stow, and take the first turning right, to Church Westcote. Follow

the road through Church Westcote to Nether Westcote (a good place for refreshments) and continue down into Idbury. Bear left at the junction for Foscot, Bledington and Kingham, winding past St Nicholas' Church. After a long descent, pass Bould Farm at Bould. Turn sharply left into Foscot, pass through the village and cross a hump-backed bridge, before turning right on to the B4450.

4 ♻ Continue, to cross the railway by Kingham Station. A little later, where the main road bends right, bear left towards Kingham. Go over the disused railway line and into Kingham. Pedal up the rise into the village, passing St Andrew's Church, and follow signs for Daylesford and

Relaxing on the green, Stow-on-the-Wold

Cornwell. Ignore the left turn to Stow and keep going straight ahead. Continue, to pass the entrance of Kingham Hill School on the right. At the crossroads, turn left to reach the A436 in ¾ mile (1km).

5 ♻ Bear left towards Stow, then take the right turn to Adlestrop. Take the first left and tour round the village, past the post office and rows of picturesque cottages. Carry on left on to the main lane, heading for Broadwell. Turn left before Evenlode, crossing the railway and the river, to reach Broadwell. Turn right into the village, signed to Stow. Go round the village green and turn left signposted 'Stow'. Follow the road past the Grange, to turn left on to the A429 into Stow-on-the-Wold. Pass through the traffic lights and turn left to return to the town square.

PLACES OF INTEREST

Stow-on-the-Wold: This quiet hill-top town – the highest in the Cotswolds – was once a busy centre of the wool industry. Its importance grew in the Middle Ages because it stood at the junction of several major routes. The large market square with its old market cross is hemmed in by a pleasing muddle of old houses and inns, and today the town is an antique hunter's paradise.

The Slaughters: These pretty Cotswold villages take their name from the Anglo-Saxon word for a muddy place, for both are threaded by picturesque streams. Upper Slaughter also has a fine Elizabethan manor house, on the left as you leave the village.

Bourton-on-the-Water: This popular beauty spot – the 'Water' is the River Windrush, which runs under little bridges beside the main street – can be admired in miniature in the gardens of The New Inn. The extensive Cotswolds Motor Museum and Toy Collection is housed in a former water mill, and is open daily from February to November. Don't miss the famous penguin tank at Birdland; many birds wander free at this marvellous garden of exotic birds (open daily, all year).

Adlestrop: Adlestrop was once the place where trains used to stop, and Edward Thomas immortalised the village in a poem of the same name. The old station sign is in the bus shelter, with a copy of the poem below it:

WHAT TO LOOK OUT FOR

Some of the churches along this route have unusual stories associated with them. Oliver Cromwell used the parish church at Stow-on-the-Wold as a temporary gaol for a thousand Royalist prisoners during the Civil War; and a hoard of Roman coins and jewellery was discovered during restoration to the church at Lower Swell. There are fine Norman carvings to be seen here, and at Upper Slaughter look for the 14th-century bellcot.

*The steam hissed. Someone
  cleared his throat.
No one left and no one came
On the bare platform. What I
  saw
Was Adlestrop – only the name.*

Jane Austen's grandfather, Thomas Leigh, was rector here and and she regularly visited the rectory, now Adlestrop House. The Leigh family have owned Adlestrop since 1553.

A narrow, sunken path leads up to the village church at Lower Slaughter

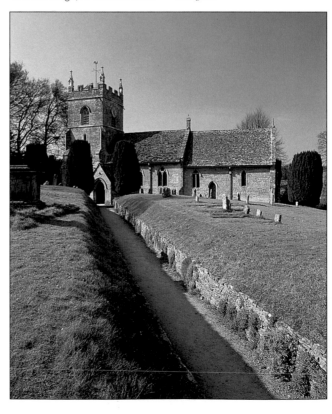

RIDE 10
WILTSHIRE
ST945295

The Nadder and Ebble Valleys

INFORMATION

Total distance
22 miles (35km)

Grade
2

OS Map
Landranger 1:50,000 sheet 184
(Salisbury & The Plain)

Nearest Railway Station
Tisbury

Cycle Shop/Hire
Just Bikes (repairs), Shaftesbury, tel:
01747 851005; Hayball & Co
(repairs /hire), Salisbury,
tel: 01722 411378; bike hire available
at The Compasses Inn, Chicksgrove,
tel: 01722 714318

The picturesque valleys of the Nadder and Ebble rivers provide the setting for a delightful ride along undulating lanes. Gentle wooded landscape and a romantic castle in the Nadder Valley contrast with the dramatic open chalk downland that flanks the narrow Ebble valley, complete with peaceful villages.

Refreshments
Pubs and a café in Tisbury.
Along the way there are The Forester
at Donhead St Andrew and
The Talbot in Berwick St John
(garden, play area),
the thatched Crown at
Alvediston (good garden), the

delightfully unspoiled Horseshoe
in Ebbesborne Wake
(pretty garden);
and the thatched and idyllically set
Compasses in Chicksgrove
welcomes children.
There are picnic spots along
the downland ridge above
Fovant

The Nadder near Sutton Mandeville

START & ROUTE DIRECTIONS

Start

The ride starts at the village of Tisbury, which lies due west of Salisbury, and 9 miles (14.5km) north-east of Shaftesbury. Park in the car park (free toilets) just east of the village centre, signed along The Avenue. Alternatively, park at Tisbury railway station.

Directions

1 ᚘ Turn left out of the car park into the village centre and turn left along the main street, soon to pass the railway station on the left. Leave the village, passing beneath the railway, then take the first turning right, signposted to Shaftesbury. Continue, parallel with the railway, and climb gradually for ¾ mile (1km), then take the lane left (unsigned), just beyond a telephone box. Ascend on a narrow lane, bearing right beside woodland, and shortly pass the driveway to Old Wardour Castle.

2 ᚘ Descend with fine views across the valley, pass the entrance to New Wardour Castle (private), then at a T-junction bear left for Shaftesbury. In ½ mile (1km) follow the lane sharp left and continue, climbing

Walking the dog in the village of Tisbury

gently, with views left across parkland towards Old Wardour Castle, to reach Donhead St Andrew. Keep to the lane through this long

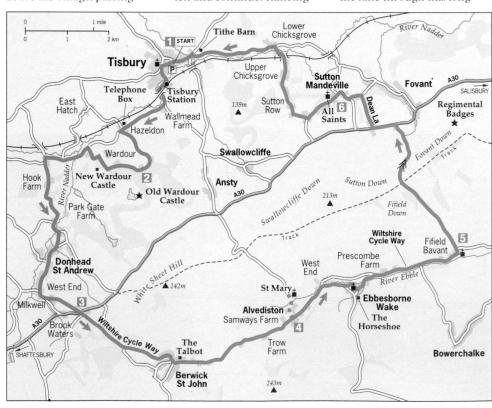

village, and continue to crossroads at the A30.

3 &dbo; Cross straight over with care, signed 'Berwick St John'. With White Sheet Hill to your left, follow this level lane (the Wiltshire Cycle Way) for 1½ miles (2.5km) into Berwick St John. Keeping left past The Talbot to begin the splendid route through the Ebble Valley. The undulating single-track lane follows the valley bottom for 2 miles (3km) into Alvediston, passing Samways Farm and the left turning (Ansty) that leads to the delightful little church of St Mary – well worth the detour.

4 &dbo; Continue for ¾ mile (1km) into the hamlet of West End and bear off right before the bridge, signed 'Ebbesborne Wake'. Shortly, keep left at a fork and drop down beside the river to enter Ebbesborne Wake. At the junction by the church, bear right for The Horseshoe pub and to explore the village; otherwise, head left out of the village and along the valley bottom. Proceed for 1½ miles (2.5km) beside the river into the hamlet of Fifield Bavant, bearing left by the church, then keep ahead at the sharp right-hand bend, signposted to Fovant.

5 &dbo; Climb steadily out of the valley, and in a mile reach the top of Fovant Down. The waymarked off-road by-way along the downland ridge is worth exploring for a good picnic site with far-reaching views. Descend the steep slope from Fovant Down to reach the A30. Turn left, and shortly turn right into Dean Lane. In ½ mile (1km) bear left, signed 'Sutton Mandeville', and climb to a junction. Keep right along Glasses Lane and enter Sutton Mandeville.

6 &dbo; Continue through the village, climbing gradually, and turn right towards Sutton Row. Beyond a sharp right-hand bend descend into the Nadder Valley and the hamlet of Upper Chicksgrove. Cross the railway and river, then at a T-junction turn left, signed 'Tisbury'. In 1½ miles (2.5km) enter the village, passing the magnificent tithe barn on the right, then shortly bear left along The Avenue to return to the car park and village.

Sheep graze in the Nadder Valley

PLACES OF INTEREST

Tisbury: This is a substantial village that has developed around the railway and is noted for its church, which dates mainly from the 13th-century and has an especially fine roof. On the eastern edge of the village is a splendid thatched 15th-century tithe barn. At nearly 200 feet in length it may be the largest in England, and forms part of medieval Place Farm, once a property of the Abbess of Shaftesbury.

Old Wardour Castle: The ruins of this unusual hexagonal building are hidden away in secluded woodland, in a truly romantic and peaceful lakeside setting. It was built in 1392 by Lord Lovel, and reconstructed in 1578 by Sir Matthew Arundell as a comfortable tower house, rather than a fortress. The castle was twice besieged and badly damaged during the Cicil War. The castle was never restored, but during the 18th century the ruins were surrounded by formal gardens (open all year).

Alvediston: An attractive small and scattered village, Alvediston is set in the upper end of the Ebble Valley. The tiny porch of St Mary's Church looks out across lush meadows, and the church itself houses numerous memorials to the Gawen and Wyndham families. Of particular note is the tomb of a knight in armour, supposedly that of John Gawen, whose family held the manor in medieval times. Sir Anthony Eden, Prime Minister between 1955 and 1957, spent his last days in the adjacent manor and is buried in the churchyard.

The ruins of Old Wardour Castle are in a particularly beautiful setting

Ebbesborne Wake: This charming unspoiled village nestles in the heart of the peaceful Ebble Valley. Neat thatched cottages congregate around the 15th-century church, which stands on a hill above the infant, crystal-clear chalk stream.

Fifield Bavant: Set just above the river meadow, this tiny hamlet comprises a few cottages, a farm complex and a delightful little church, which enjoys an idyllic view along this tranquil valley. It could well be the smallest parish church in Wiltshire, and has a 13th-century lancet window and a Norman font. Its only access is through the farmyard.

The by-way along the chalk ridge top is known as the Salisbury Way, and is an ancient route linking Salisbury to the West Country. Evidence of its early importance can be traced through the presence of earthworks, barrows and an Iron Age settlement.

WHAT TO LOOK OUT FOR

Tisbury churchyard is worth a visit to see its massive yew tree, which is reputedly more than a thousand years old. Look more closely to find the graves of Rudyard Kipling and his parents.

Unusually, the churchyard at Ebbesborne Wake is a Wildlife Conservation Area. Here, grasses are left long to help them seed and butterflies to breed, and both gravestones and walls are left untouched to preserve mosses.

All Saints Church in Sutton Mandeville has a beautifully carved Jacobean pulpit, and the churchyard is home to a rare sundial with a ball top, set on a stone monument dated 1685.

After your rapid descent from Fovant Down, take time to observe the huge regimental badges carved in the chalk hillside by soldiers stationed in Fovant during World War I.

Brockenhurst: New Forest Heathland

RIDE 11
HAMPSHIRE
SU304031

INFORMATION

Total Distance
23½ miles (37.5km), with 6½ miles (10.5km) off-road

Grade
2

OS Maps
Landranger 1:50,000 sheet 196 (Solent & The Isle of Wight)

Tourist Information
Lyndhurst, tel: 01703 282269

Cycle Shop/Hire
New Forest Cycle Experience, Brockenhurst, tel: 01590 624204; Hollands Wood Forestry Commission Campsite Cycle Hire (entrance off A337, just north

A delightful ride through peaceful New Forest heathland and inclosures via excellent gravel tracks and along gently rolling Forest fringe lanes, with views across the Solent to the Isle of Wight. As well as a wealth of woodland wildlife, added attractions include the National Motor Museum at Beaulieu and the historic village of Bucklers Hard, making this an interesting and varied day out.

of The Balmer Lawn Hotel), open during the summer season

Nearest Railway Station
Brockenhurst

Refreshments
Brockenhurst is well supplied with pubs, hotel bars and tea rooms, notably The Thatched Cottage Hotel

The ponies which roam freely are an integral part of the New Forest

for light lunches and teas. Along the route, both Beaulieu and Bucklers Hard have a tea room and pub (open all day in summer, garden, and children welcomed); at Pilley, The Fleur de Lys offers a pleasant garden and a warm welcome to families; restaurant and café at the National Motor Museum, Beaulieu. Picnic beside forest tracks or the Beaulieu River in Buckler's Hard. Toilets at Hatchet Pond, Beaulieu, Buckler's Hard and Brockenhurst

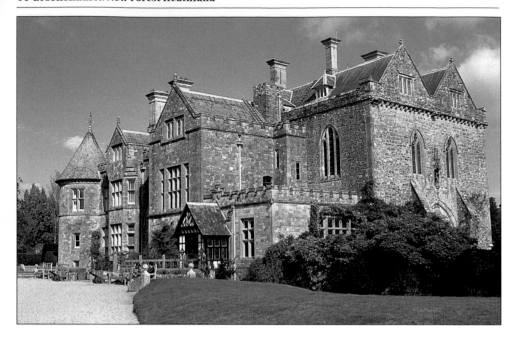

The historic house of Beaulieu, home to generations of Montagus, was originally the gatehouse of a great abbey

Start

Brockenhurst is situated on the A337, midway between Lyndhurst and Lymington and 7 miles (11km) south of junction 1 of the M27 at Cadnam. Park at the Balmerlawn Forestry Commission car park (free) at the junction of the A337 and B3055, just north of the village.

Directions

1 🚲 Leave the car park and turn right along the B3055 through Balmerlawn, then after ¼ mile (0.5km) bear off left on to a good gravel track (arrowed 'Car Park') across heathland. Pass Tilery Lane car park and soon curve left

to the small car park at Standing Hat. Keep right, pass beside a barrier and shortly go through a gate, skirting the grounds of a woodland cottage. Proceed along a forest track to reach a crossing of tracks (post with yellow badge D12) and turn right towards a gate and soon cross a bridge over the railway.

2 🚲 Take the first track left, then after ½ mile (1km) turn right at a crossing of five ways (deer research sign) and follow a gently ascending track to a gate. Bear left to a further gate, then descend to a crossing of tracks and turn left. Keep left uphill where a track merges from the right and remain on this quiet forest track for ¾ mile (1km) to a gate beyond a

brook. Climb a heathland track, then bear right to merge with a metalled lane at Furzey Lodge and soon reach a crossroads at Hatchet Pond.

3 🚲 Turn left along the B3054 (taking great care, as this can be busy, especially in summer) for 1 mile (1.5km) and turn right, signposted 'Bucklers Hard'. Continue downhill for 200yds (192m) and turn right, to visit Beaulieu Village. Keep to the B-road for a further ½ mile (1km) to reach the entrance for the National Motor Museum and Beaulieu Abbey. Follow the lane uphill and keep left with 'Bucklers Hard' signs for 2 miles (3km) to reach the historic village.

4 🚲 Continue along the narrow lane (Solent Way) to

[Map showing Brockenhurst and New Forest Heathland area with locations including Lyndhurst, Standing Hat, Balmerlawn, Brockenhurst Station, Brockenhurst, Roydon Wood Nature Reserve, Setley, Sandy Down, Boldre Church, Boldre, Pilley Bailey, Bull Hill, Fleur de Lys, Pilley, Portmore, Lymington, Furzey Lodge, Hatchet Pond, Hatchet Gate, East Boldre, Beaulieu Heath, Norleywood, Beck Farm, East End, National Motor Museum, Beaulieu Abbey, Beaulieu, Beufre Farm, Bucklers Hard, Clobb, Tithe Barn & Chapel, Bergerie, St Leonards Grange, New Milton, Setley Plain. Routes numbered 1 START, 2, 3, 4, 5, 6.]

a T-junction. Turn left, signed 'St Leonards', and shortly pass the ruins of a tithe barn and a chapel. Bear right and proceed along this level lane, with views across the Solent to the Isle of Wight; keep straight on at the next two junctions to reach the hamlet of East End after 1 mile (1.5km). Keep left at a junction, then in 100yds (91m) turn right, signed 'Norleywood'. Remain on this narrow lane through the hamlet to reach the B3054.

5 🚲 Cross over in to Bull Hill, signposted 'Pilley'. Proceed through Pilley Bailey, then just before reaching The Fleur de Lys pub, turn right opposite the Memorial Hall into Church Lane. After ¾ mile (1km) reach the isolated and interesting Boldre Church. Descend, ignore the turning left and soon cross the Lymington River. At a

crossroads, turn right along a 'No Through Road', which soon becomes a gravel bridleway through Roydon Wood Nature Reserve.

6 🚲 Keep to the main gravel bridleway as it bears left through the woodland. Cross a cattle grid, pass a house and keep left to reach the A337. Cross over with care, signed

'Sway', and cross Setley Plain. Shortly, turn right on to the B3055 (Brockenhurst) and after a mile (1.5km) reach the centre of the village. Go straight on at a crossroads, then turn left on reaching the A337 for the short ride back to the Balmerlawn car park.

Beaulieu village church

PLACES OF INTEREST

New Forest: Created as a royal hunting ground by William the Conqueror more than 900 years ago, the area comprises some 92,000 acres (37,000ha) of undulating forest and heathland threaded by small streams and scattered with ponds.

Beaulieu: The 16th-century house, set beside the Beaulieu river, is only the gatehouse to a great abbey that once existed and has been in the Montagu family since 1538.
It is also home to the world's largest collection of vehicles, motoring memorabilia, a model railway, monorail and various events (open every day of the year).

Bucklers Hard: This picturesque small Beaulieu

Houses lead down to the water at Bucklers Hard

River village thrived for centuries as a shipbuilding yard and Nelson's fleet was built here. A fascinating little maritime museum recalls this tradition and cottage displays recreate 18th-century life.

Boldre Church: Standing isolated in the forest, St John's church is of interest, not only for its pleasing location, but for the memorials inside to HMS *Hood*, the warship that sank in 1941 killing 1,416 men. They include a painting of the ship, a few lanterns and two carved benches in the south porch. The Vice-Admiral had been a regular worshipper at the church.

Roydon Wood Nature Reserve: Occupying 700 acres (280ha) of mixed woodland, heathland and meadow in the Lymington river valley, it is haven to many species of fauna and flora, including 29 species of butterfly, in addition to foxes, badgers, deer, nightjars, scrub warblers and various owls.

WHAT TO LOOK OUT FOR

Some 2,000 deer roam freely throughout much of the New Forest, so keep an eye open for herds of fallow deer and in this particular area you may well see red, roe and sika deer grazing along the grassy forest rides.
Look out for green woodpeckers which feed on the wood ants along the gravel tracks, and for some of the 3,500 ponies which live semi-wild on the open heathlands.
The mixed woodland at Roydon Wood Nature Reserve is carpeted with bluebells in spring.

Tidal Creeks and Chalk Downland

RIDE 12
ISLE OF WIGHT
SZ353896

INFORMATION

Total Distance
21 miles (33.5km) with 4½ miles
(7km) off-road

Grade
2 (3 if following the Tennyson Trail
over Compton Down)

OS Maps
Landranger 1:50,000 sheet 196
(Solent & The Isle of Wight)

Tourist Information
Yarmouth (summer only),
tel: 01983 760015;
Newport, tel: 01983 525450

Cycle Shops/Hire
Isle Cycle Hire (Wavells Fine Foods),

By following a pleasant mixture of B-roads, quiet narrow lanes, scenic downland tracks and a splendid former railway route beside the River Yar, this ride explores every facet of the island, from wildlife-rich river creeks and lofty chalk downland with majestic views to charming unspoiled villages. Take your time, as there is much to explore and the downland climbs, although short, are quite challenging – the effort will be well rewarded.

Yarmouth, tel: 01983 760219; Mobile
Cycle Service (hire & repairs), Thorley,
tel: 01983 760818

Refreshments
There are several pubs, cafés and the
Jerih Tea Rooms in Yarmouth.
Two good pubs on the route, The

New Inn, Shalfleet, and Sun Inn,
Hulverstone, are open all day in
summer and welcome children. The
Sun Inn, Calbourne (play area) is also
a good place to stop.
Plenty of picnic places
at Brighstone Down (official), or
anywhere on the chalk downs,
and benches beside the
River Yar.

Newtown Quay

START & ROUTE DIRECTIONS

Start

Yarmouth is an historic small town located on the west side of the island on the A3054 Newport to Totland road, 9 miles (14.5km) west of Newport. Parking available in River Road pay and display car park, a short distance from the ferry terminal. Easily accessible from the mainland via the regular Lymington to Yarmouth ferry (bikes free).

Directions

1 🚲 Turn right out of the car park and follow the A3054 for ½ mile (1km), with fine views across the Solent, and turn right on to Thorley Road (B3401). After ½ mile (1km) bear left with the B-road, signed to Thorley and Wellow, and remain on this generally level road for 2 miles (3km) to reach a T-junction beyond Wellow. Turn left along Station Road, then in 200yds (192m) take the right turn towards Shalfleet.

2 🚲 Follow this narrow lane into Shalfleet, passing the post office and store, to reach the A3054. Turn right downhill to the traffic lights and The New Inn and turn left if wishing to explore Shalfleet Quay and Creek. Otherwise, continue straight uphill and bear left just before the petrol station, signed 'Newtown'. In ½ mile (1km), turn left for Newtown and shortly cross a bridge over

Attractive cottages are almost smothered by lush vegetation in Winkle Street, Calbourne

Newtown Brook, with the tidal creek and nature reserve to your left. Gradually ascend into Newtown and pass the Old Town Hall. Turn left here to explore the hamlet and the old quay.

3 🚲 Follow the road right in Newtown and continue for ¾ mile (1km) to reach a staggered crossroads. Go straight across, signed 'Watchingwell'. Follow this narrow lane to the A3054 and turn right, then shortly bear off left along Pound Lane towards Five Houses. After 1 mile (1.5km) reach a crossroads, turn left for Calbourne and gently ascend to a crossroads with the B3401, beside the popular Sun Inn.

4 🚲 Go straight over into picturesque Calbourne,

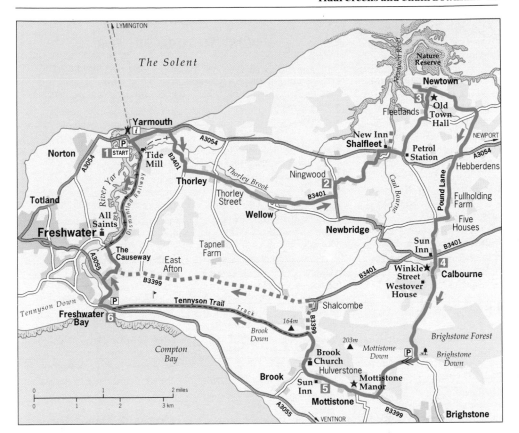

pass Winkle Street and
Westover House and begin
a gradual climb towards
Brighstone Down. The road
enters Brighstone Forest
and ascends steeply to
Mottistone Down (NT). Take
the narrow lane on the right
(opposite the track to the
picnic area) and descend
quickly on this scenic rolling
lane to reach the B3399.
Turn right (unsigned) and
go through Mottistone to
reach Hulverstone.

5 🚲 Pass the Sun Inn and
remain on the B3399 to pass
Brook church. Climb steadily
for ¼ mile (0.5km) to turn left
onto a waymarked bridle

road, signed 'Freshwater'.
Go through a gate then
ascend steeply (this may
necessitate walking bikes) up
a dry chalk track for a short
distance to the top of Brook
Down, for breathtaking
views across Freshwater Bay
to Tennyson Down. Remain
on this good track (the
Tennyson Trail) across open
downland for 1½ miles
(2.5km) before descending
steadily to a car park and
the A3055.
(*Alternatively*, if it is very
breezy, stay on the B3399
westwards for 3 miles (5km)
and turn right to rejoin the
route on The Causeway,
signed 'Freshwater'.)

6 🚲 Turn right, steeply
downhill into Freshwater Bay
and follow the A3055 right
(inland) to go through
Freshwater. Turn right for a
short distance along the
B3399, then shortly turn left
along The Causeway, signed
to Freshwater. On reaching
the River Yar, turn right
along the dismantled railway
(with All Saints Church
across the river), then after
1½ miles (2.5km) on nearing
Yarmouth, bear left alongside
the river towards the Tide
Mill. Keep straight on along
Mill Lane to the A3054 in
Yarmouth and turn left to
return to the starting point
and car park .

PLACES OF INTEREST

Yarmouth: An interesting and picturesque little town situated on the River Yar with stone quays, old houses and a harbour full of boats. The Tudor castle, tucked away down a passage, was built by Henry VIII after the French had sacked the town in 1524. It is no ruin – visitors can see the Master Gunner's parlour and kitchen, plus an unusually small great hall.

Shalfleet: Located at the head of the Newtown river estuary, this little village has a 17th-century quay built of huge boulders. Once used for unloading coal, the only boats that come and go now are yachts and dinghies in this peaceful, wildlife-rich area of creeklands.

Newtown: Unbelievably, this creekside hamlet was the capital of the Isle of Wight and is the most ancient of the island boroughs. The 17th-century town hall stands as a monument to Newtown's past importance; it witnessed many parliamentary elections. The harbour once sheltered great masted ships and supported an oyster industry, but today the mudflats are home to a wide variety of birds.

Calbourne: One of the most beautiful villages on the island, notable for its Winkle Street, a picturesque row of thatched cottages opposite a stream.

All Saints Church, Yarmouth

WHAT TO LOOK OUT FOR

Both the Yar and Newtown river estuaries are a birdwatcher's delight with wintering brent geese and shelduck swelling the numbers of more common species – curlew, oystercatchers, teal and herons – so take your binoculars! Along the old railway line beside the River Yar warblers and nightingales can be seen and heard among the reedbeds in summer. Primroses abound along the roadside verges and the chalk downland is a haven for rock roses, horseshoe vetch and autumn gentian, among other plants. Thirty species of butterfly can be seen, including the dark green fritillary. In Newtown look out for the ancient coat of arms above the door to a house called 'Noah's Ark', which was a pub until 1913.

Brighstone Forest and Mottistone Down: The largest area of forest on the island where red squirrels and badgers are among the wildlife to be seen. Mottistone Down rises to 666ft (203m) and on the chalk ridge are a number of ancient burial grounds or tumuli dating back to the early Bronze Age.

Mottistone Manor Garden: Colourful herbaceous borders, flowering fruit trees and delightful sea views combine to make a perfect setting for this fine 16th- and 17th-century stone manor house which overlooks the partly 12th-century church and the village green.

All Saints Church, Freshwater: Freshwater was the home of Alfred Lord Tennyson and his wife Emily from 1853 to their respective deaths in 1892 and 1896. Emily is buried in the churchyard, and various memorials decorate the interior walls. The church stands on a hillock overlooking the River Yar.

Odiham: The Basingstoke Canal

This interesting and varied ride incorporates the peaceful towpath beside the Basingstoke Canal, scenic tracks, undulating lanes and attractive villages. It is generally easy-going, off-road biking, with the exception of one stony section of by-way. Take care with children alongside the canal!

INFORMATION

Total distance
22 miles (35km),
with 10½ miles (17km) off-road

Grade
2

OS Maps
Landranger 1:50,000 sheet 186
(Aldershot & Guildford)

Tourist Information
Basingstoke, tel: 01256 817618

Cycle Shops/Hire
None on route

Nearest Railway Station
Hook (3 miles 4.5km)

Refreshments
There are various tea rooms,
hotels and pubs in Odiham, including
The Waterwitch pub
with a canalside garden/play area.
Along the way, try
The Fox and Goose at Greywell
(play area), or
The Barley Mow Tea Rooms
at Winchfield Hurst;
The Hoddington Arms at
Upton Grey and
The Chequers at Well
both offer good food and
welcome families.
There are also plenty of picnic spots
along the canal

A scenic swing-bridge on the Basingstoke Canal

START & ROUTE DIRECTIONS

Start

Odiham lies just off the B3349 between Reading and Alton, 2 miles (3km) from junction 5 of the M3. Begin the ride from Odiham Wharf canalside car park (free) at Colt Hill, north of the High Street. The canal is signposted.

Directions

1 Join the canal towpath, turn right beneath the road bridge with The Waterwitch pub across the canal to your left. Proceed along this picturesque stretch of the Basingstoke Canal on a good towpath for 2 miles (3km), passing through North Warnborough and beside the splendid ruin of King John's Castle to reach the village of Greywell, just beyond the entrance to Greywell Tunnel.

2 Turn right along Deptford Lane, then almost immediately bear left at a T-junction along The Street, signposted 'Up Nately'. Leave the village, pass a lane on the left, then in a short distance bear off left onto a waymarked concrete by-way towards farm buildings. Shortly, keep right along a grass-centred track that climbs gently uphill to a junction of five ways among beech trees – Five Lanes End – affording open views north.

3 Keep left, pass a barn on the right, then turn left along a good surfaced track to reach a metalled lane by a house. Turn right, then at a T-junction bear left downhill through Upton Grey to a further T-junction beside the duckpond. Turn left, then right before The Hoddington Arms, signed 'South Warnborough'. Continue for 1½ miles (2.5km) on an undulating lane into the village.

4 Cross the B3346 with care to join a narrow rolling

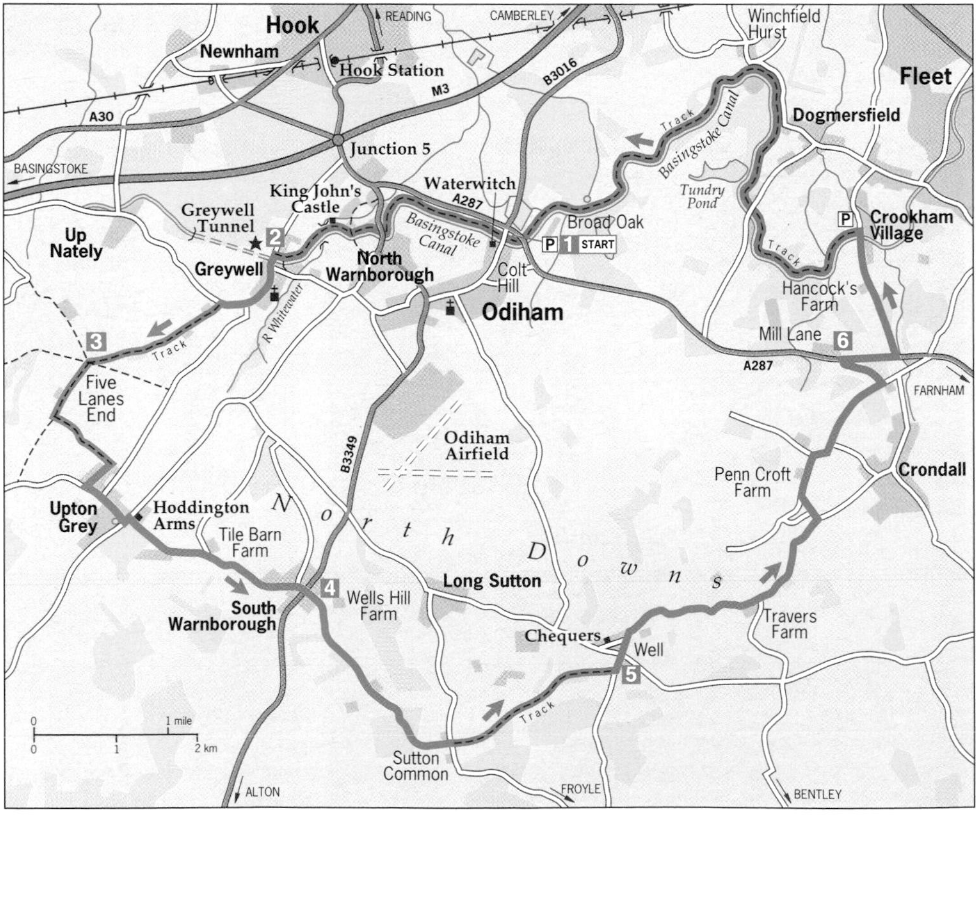

lane, signposted 'Froyle'. In 1¼ miles (3km) at a T-junction of lanes at Sutton Common, go straight ahead onto a waymarked, hedged track. Keep to this green lane (stony in places) for just over a mile to reach a lane, and turn left into the hamlet of Well.

5 🚲 At the crossroads go straight over, then soon keep right for Crondall. After 1¼ miles (2km), disregard the lane arrowed to 'Bentley', then beyond a sharp right-hand bend take the next unsigned lane left (signed 'Countryscene Hand-made Rugs'). Ignoring lanes to the left and right, proceed for 1 mile (1.5km) to a T-junction at a grass triangle, and bear left into the hamlet of Mill Lane. Turn left at the next T-junction, then shortly turn

right onto the busy A287 (take great care), signposted to Farnham.

6 🚲 In 200yds (185m) bear off left for Crookham Village. Continue for a mile (1.5km), cross the Basingstoke Canal and immediately turn left into Crookham Wharf car park to rejoin the canal towpath.

Greywell Tunnel is a bat haven

Remain on the delightful tree-shaded towpath (some gates) beside the peacefully meandering canal for 6 miles (10km), through Dogmersfield and Winchfield Hurst, back to the car park at Odiham Wharf.

Blossom on Odiham high street

PLACES OF INTEREST

Odiham: Despite the presence of the fast-expanding towns of Aldershot and Basingstoke, Odiham retains a distinct country atmosphere.

Its attractive High Street is mainly Georgian in character and the town also boasts a Tudor vicarage and a fine 14th-century church, the largest in North Hampshire, which contains an impressive carved pulpit, a 17th-century gallery staircase and a 13th-century chalk font. In the churchyard stands a curious old 'Pest House', built to house the victims of the Great Plague in 1665.

Basingstoke Canal: Originally conceived as a major commercial route between London and North Hampshire, it was completed in 1794 and climbed 37 miles through Surrey to Hampshire with the aid of 29 locks. Barges transported timber, coal and grain, but the development of the railways led to the gradual decline of the canal as a commercial route. In 1966 the Surrey and Hampshire Canal Society began to restore the canal, and in 1991 32 miles (49km) from the River Wey navigation to the Greywell Tunnel were re-opened as a leisure amenity.

King John's Castle: Also known as Odiham Castle, it was built in 1212 and it was from here that King John set out for Runnymede in 1215 to sign the Magna Carta. The only remaining part of the castle today is its intriguing octagonal-shaped keep.

Greywell: An enchanting village of mainly 17th-century brick and timber cottages, with a fine medieval church standing close to the River Whitewater. Greywell Tunnel was built in 1792 and at 1,230yds (1,125m) was the longest canal tunnel in southern

Cycling along the towpath at North Warnborough

England. Since its collapse in 1934 it has become one of the most important bat roosts in Britain, with an estimated 2,000 bats and five different species, including the natterer's bat.

WHAT TO LOOK OUT FOR

Basingstoke Canal is an important freshwater wildlife habitat and the towpath is a particularly good place for bird-watching, notably for wagtails, moorhens, mallards, herons and the blue flash of the kingfisher. Swallows and house martins find rich feeding on the wing and numerous warblers and flycatchers nest in the undergrowth in the summer. Dragonflies, frogs and water voles are a common sight and if lucky you may spot a pike swimming in the shallows. Dusk is the time to be at the entrance to Greywell Tunnel, to see the large number of bats leaving the tunnel to feed.

RIDE 14
WEST SUSSEX
SU977217

Petworth and the Arun Valley

This route offers a not-too-energetic ride through the Arun Valley and along undulating lanes at the base of the majestic South Downs. It is mainly on quiet, narrow lanes, with a short stretch of busy A-road. Attractions along the way range from nature reserves to a splendid Roman villa.

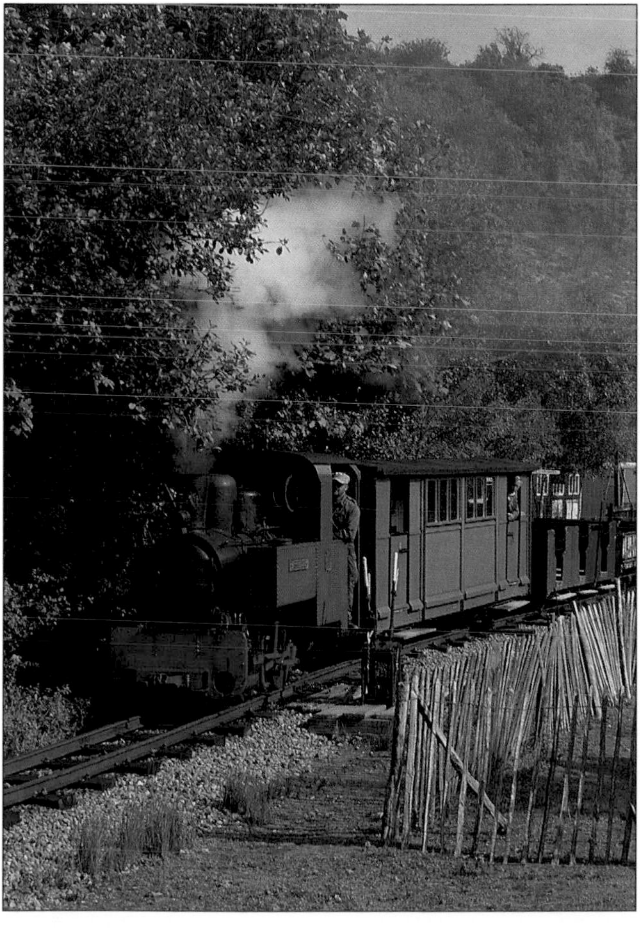

INFORMATION

Total Distance
22 miles (35km)

Grade
2

OS Map
Landranger 1:50,000 sheet 197 (Chichester & The Downs)

Tourist Information
Petworth, tel: 01798 343230

Cycle Shop/Hire
Weald Bicycles, Midhurst, tel: 01730 815656

Nearest Railway Station
Amberley (on route); Pulborough (2 miles/3km east of Fittleworth)

Refreshments
Good range of cafés and pubs in Petworth, especially Petworth House restaurant (NT – free admission). On the route try The Swan in Fittleworth (open all day, play area), the welcoming White Horse in Sutton (garden) or The Black Horse at Amberley; children welcome at The Bridge Inn, beside the River Arun. Café and picnic area at Amberley Museum; teas and toilets at the RSPB Nature Reserve; café at the Roman Villa, Bignor

Amberley Museum is just one of the attractions along the route

START & ROUTE DIRECTIONS

Start

Petworth is a small market town with attractive timbered houses located on the A272, between Billingshurst and Midhurst. Park in the car park south of the market square (well signed).

Directions

1️⃣ 🚲 Leave the car park and follow the one-way system left, then turn right to skirt the wall of Petworth Park. Just beyond the church, bear right into East Street, signed to Pulborough. Go straight over the crossroads into Middle Street, and shortly turn left along the High Street and leave the town. In ¾ mile (1km) turn left at a T-junction, and after about a mile reach the A283.

2️⃣ 🚲 Bear right on to the main road, signed 'Pulborough', and take the first lane off to the right, to skirt Hesworth Common. Descend sharply, keeping left, then bear right at a fork. Enter Lower Fittleworth, and

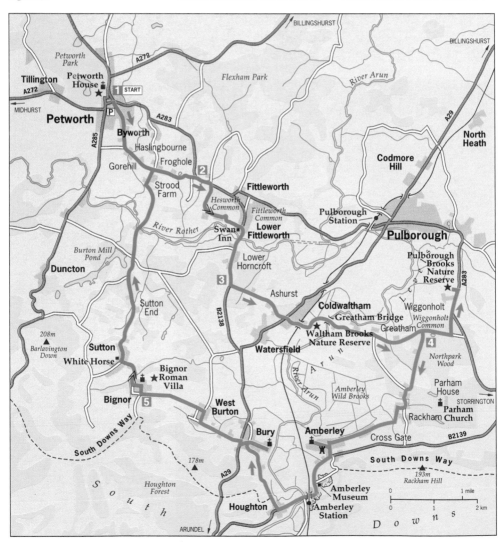

reach the B2138 by The Swan Inn. Turn right, cross the River Rother and continue straight on, to turn left, signed 'Coldwaltham'.

3 🚲 Continue for 1 mile (1.5km), to meet the A29. Go straight over, towards Greatham. Leave Coldwaltham, cross the railway and River Arun and follow a good level road across the Arun floodplain, passing through Greatham. To visit Pulborough Brooks Nature Reserve go straight on and turn left through Wiggonholt Common to reach the A283. Bear left, and turn left beyond the turning to Wiggonholt village for the RSPB Reserve. Retrace the route across Wiggonholt Common, turning right at the T-junction, then take the first lane left, signed 'Rackham'.

4 🚲 Proceed through Northpark Wood, pass Parham church, then turn right towards Amberley. Follow the undulating lane, with views across the Arun Levels, for 1 mile (1.5km) into Amberley. At a sharp left-hand bend, turn right to explore the attractive village and church. Otherwise, continue left, to reach the B2139. Turn right here and gradually descend to Amberley station, passing Amberley Museum. Continue on this road into Houghton and turn right, signposted to Bury. Follow the rolling lane for 1 mile (1.5km) into Bury, turning right at the crossroads to see the church, and for access to the banks of

Looking out for spring arrivals at Pulborough Brooks Nature Reserve

the River Arun. Return to the crossroads, keep straight on to the busy A29; turn right, then immediately left towards West Burton. Follow this undulating road, and bear right, then left, through West Burton, towards Bignor. Pass the entrance to Bignor Roman Villa on the right.

5 🚲 In a short distance bear right and soon left through the village, and keep straight on at the junction by the church, towards Sutton.

Descend a steep hill with care, and gradually ascend into Sutton, following the lane right in front of The White Horse. Remain on this lane for 1½ miles (2.5km) to a crossroads. Go straight over, signed to Byworth, and shortly cross the River Rother. In a further mile turn left at a staggered crossroads to rejoin the outward route back into Petworth and the car park.

Petworth House is set in parkland

PLACES OF INTEREST

Petworth: Petworth is dominated by the huge 17th-century mansion of Petworth House set in a vast walled and landscaped deer park. The west front is 320ft (97.5m) long; behind it are rooms full of art treasures including paintings by Turner and Gainsborough, and Grinling Gibbons' extraordinary carvings.
The little town seems to crowd around the gate; narrow winding streets lead off the tiny market place. Notable buildings include the arcaded 18th-century town hall.

Pulborough Brooks Nature Reserve (RSPB): Tucked away near the tiny hamlet of Wiggonholt on the edge of the Arun Levels, the reserve has a visitor centre in a beautifully restored barn (free entry) with displays, games play area and garden. There are also wildlife walks, viewpoints and observation hides (open daily).

Amberley: Set on a low ridge overlooking the area know as Amberley Wild Brooks, Amberley is a picturesque jumble of old thatched houses and charming gardens. The castle was built in 1380 for the Bishops of Chichester, and damaged during the Civil War. The ruined gatehouse and walls enclose an ancient manor house, now an exclusive hotel. In the church, red ochre wall paintings date from about 1200.
Amberley Museum is a lively, working museum celebrating local crafts and industries. Here you can visit craftsmen –

WHAT TO LOOK OUT FOR

Amberley Wild Brooks is a nature reserve comprising a network of small watercourses and meadows, which are usually flooded in the winter. After crossing the River Arun, it is worth exploring the footpath off the lane through Waltham Brooks Nature Reserve. The area is a superb feeding and breeding habitat for wildfowl and waders, notably in winter for the large flock of Bewick swans that roost here. Snipe, lapwings, redshank, shelduck, mallard and yellow wagtail nest among the tussocky grass, and swallows and house martins hunt over the open waters in summer.
Look out for two memorial plaques along the way. On the churchyard wall at Amberley is a plaque to the famous artist Arthur Rackham and his wife who lived and worked in nearby Houghton House. In Bury, the handsome Tudor-style mansion of Bury House sports a plaque to John Galsworthy (1867–1933), author of *The Forsyte Saga*, who lived the last seven years of his life in the house.

blacksmith, potter, printer or boat-builder – and experience the sights, sounds and smells of their workshops. Other exhibits include vintage buses and a narrow gauge railway (open from March to October).

Bignor Roman Villa: Situated in a superb rural location below the South Downs, this Roman house – one of the largest known – was rediscovered in 1811. In its heyday it consisted of almost 70 buildings. Displayed under cover are some of the finest mosaics in the country: the 80ft (24.5m) long mosaic in the north corridor is particularly spectacular. The underfloor heating system can be clearly seen, and the museum contains many interesting artefacts found on the site (open on most days from March to October).

Hesworth Common

Hailsham, Alfriston and The Cuckoo Trail

This is a scenic figure-of-eight route which can be ridden as two separate rides of about equal length, leading from the meandering reed-lined lanes of the Pevensey levels to picturesque villages tucked under the Downs. The off-road sections are on good forest tracks and along a railway path.

RIDE 15
EAST SUSSEX
TQ592095

INFORMATION

Total Distance
28 miles (45km),
with 3½ miles (5.5km) off-road

Grade
2

OS Map
Landranger 1:50,000 sheet 199
(Eastbourne & Hastings)

Tourist Information
Hailsham, tel: 01323 442667;
Pevensey, tel: 01323 761444

Cycle Shops
Chris Pellings, Hailsham, tel: 01323
840601; Kontour Cycles, Polegate
(01323 482368); Cuckmere Cycle
Company (hire), Alfriston, tel: 01323
870310

Nearest Railway Station
Polegate (3 miles/5km)

Refreshments
Pubs and tea room in Hailsham and
Pevensey, and including
Ye Olde Smugglers Inne at Alfriston;
also Giants Rest pub at Wilmington,
The Yew Tree at Arlington, and
Loom Mill on the Cuckoo Trail.
Pub and café at Drusillas Zoo Park
(access free)

The church of St Nicholas, Pevensey

START & ROUTE DIRECTIONS

Start

Hailsham is on the A295, just off the A22, some 7 miles (11.5km) north of Eastbourne. Park in the town centre; the route starts from the southern end of the High Street.

Directions

1 🚲 From the bottom of the High Street (one way), at the corner of Market Square, proceed into Mill Road. Continue for 1 mile (1.5km) to a junction, and turn left, signposted 'Pevensey'. After ½ mile (1km) turn left and follow signs for Pevensey through Downash to Rickney Farm, with fine views of Herstmonceux Church and the old telescope buildings of the former observatory to the left. Continue on this road, meandering between water-filled dykes with views of the Downs and the outlines of Pevensey Castle.

2 🚲 Turn right at a junction, and at the roundabout take the third exit to Pevensey. Go through traffic lights into the High Street, in a short distance, turn left into an alley beside Pevensey Courthouse to the church of St Nicolas, and turn right to see the castle. Leave by the West Gate and go into Westham High Street. Part way along, at a car park sign, turn right into

The George Inn is one of Alfriston's many fine timbered buildings

Peelings Lane. In ½ mile (1km) at the crossroads, turn right up a hill, and go over the bypass towards Hankham. In the village, turn right at The Dog House, and in ½ mile (1km) where the road heads right, keep left, signposted to Hailsham. The Downs, destination of the second loop of the ride, are clearly visible as the B2104 is reached.

3 🚲 Turn right on to the B2104, and in ½ mile (1km), go left into Ottham Court Lane. After a mile, turn right on to the Cuckoo Trail, along a former railway line. Stay on the trail, passing the Loom Mill Craft Centre into Hailsham. (Turn left at the Common Pond, and continue to the end of Station Road to

return to the town centre.) At the Cuckoo Trail car park, turn left along South Road. Go straight on over a mini-roundabout, and in ½ mile (1km), at Cacklebury stores, turn right up Arlington Road East to meet the A22. Keep left on the shared footway to cross the A22 with care, into Arlington Road West, and immediately turn left into Robin Post Lane.

4 🚲 Continue straight ahead on to a track which goes through Wilmington Forest (after 1½ miles/2.5km this becomes a metalled surface). At the end of the lane, follow signs to Wilmington, with an excellent view of the chalk Long Man as you cross the common. Cross the A27 with care, and continue into Wilmington. Beyond the village, at the top of a hill, the Long Man car park marks a footpath up to the chalk figure. Continue on this road – a steady climb to the top of the hill gives extensive views across the Cuckmere valley and to Arlington Reservoir. On the descent, High and Over Hill with its white horse can be seen. Part way down the hill a footpath to the right leads to the tiny church of Lullington. Turn right at the foot of the hill, signposted 'Alfriston', and in ½ mile (1km), at Plonks Barn, turn left on to a bridleway over the Cuckmere River into Alfriston. Keep right at the Market Cross and follow the valley northwards, passing Drusillas Zoo Park. Cross the A27 at the roundabout, and in 1 mile (1.5km) at cross-roads turn right, signposted to Arlington. (Keep straight on for the picnic area by Arlington Reservoir.)

5 🚲 Skirting the reservoir, continue on this road through Arlington Village. Pass The Yew Tree Inn and continue to Abbots Wood (entrance on the right). After another mile, bear right towards Hailsham (or turn left here to visit Michelham Priory). Continue to meet and cross the A22, and retrace the route back into Hailsham town centre.

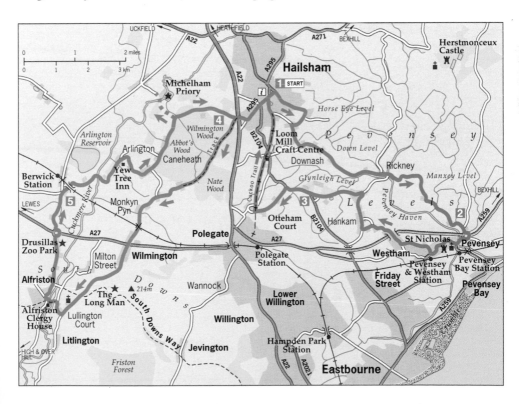

The Long Man, or Wilmington Giant, is a famous landmark

PLACES OF INTEREST

Hailsham: This old town's tradition of rope-making is reflected in the names of some of the streets and alleys, and this is where the hangman's rope was manufactured. While rope is still made here today, the town's more recent claim to fame is in its role on the route of the Cuckoo Trail, the first stage of a proposed long-distance cycleway, which already gives 11 miles (17.5km) of superb off-road riding on the old railway line between Polegate and Heathfield.

Pevensey and Westham: The two attractive, half-timbered villages are situated at opposite gateways of the old Roman fort of Anderida.
William, Duke of Normandy landed near Pevensey in 1066, and a Norman keep was built within the walls of the old Roman fort by William's half-brother, Robert of Mortain. The castle had mixed fortunes and several owners throughout its history, and was beseiged on a number of occasions, most famously after the Battle of Lewes in 1264–5. Today, later additions to the fortifications of Pevensey Castle can be admired, including cunningly hidden defences from World War II (open all year, but not on winter Mondays and Tuesdays).

Wilmington: The chalk figure of the Long Man (also known as the Wilmington Giant) dominates this little village, and some say it dates back to Viking times. Long barrows and ancient tumuli are scattered on the hillside above.

Alfriston: The gem of the downland villages is set in the lovely Cuckmere Valley. The 14th-century thatched Clergy House, on The Tye, was the first building acquired by the National Trust in 1896, but there many more old houses to be seen in the narrow High Street. Near by, Lullington church is one of England's smallest – don't miss it. Drusillas Park just outside the town, is a famous small-scale zoo-park and gardens, with many attractions including otters, flamingos and meerkats. There's also an adventure playground, and the park is open all year round.

Michelham Priory: An Augustinian priory was founded here in 1229, and the site includes a 14th-century gatehouse and a 16th-century house with interesting furniture, stained glass and tapestries. There is a fascinating physic garden, and a working watermill (all attractions open in summer).

WHAT TO LOOK OUT FOR

The Pevensey Levels are a favourite spot for migrating birds, including fieldfares and plovers.
Swans and ducks nest here, too. Among the birds on Arlington Reservoir, watch for grey herons.
Wild flowers associated with the chalky Downs flourish in late spring – look out especially for the bright yellow cowslips near the Long Man of Wilmington.
On the Cuckoo Trail, look out for the metal sculptures which adorn the road crossing points.

Penshurst and Tudor Kent

The ride through this Tudor-influenced part of Kent is pleasant and historically interesting. Some short hills provide height for views over the surrounding countryside, and the suddenly encountered outcrops of rock seem out of place in this type of terrain. The route is on-road, with the option of a short bridleway run at the end for off-road cycling.

INFORMATION

Total distance
16 miles (25.5km),
with an optional 1½ miles (2.5km)
off-road

Grade
2

OS Maps
Landranger 1:50,000 sheet 188
(Maidstone & The Weald of Kent)

Tourist information
Tonbridge, tel: 01732 770929

Cycle hire
Fir Tree House Tea Rooms, Penshurst,
tel: 01892 870382

Nearest railway station
Penshurst (2 miles/3km)

Refreshments
Plenty of facilities in Penshurst,
including the
Fir Tree House Tea Rooms,
Quaintways, The Leicester Arms pub,
and The Spotted Dog.
Pubs on the route include The
Fountain at Cowden (no facilities for
children), The Kentish Horse at
Markbeech, The Henry VIII at Hever,
The Wheatsheaf at Bough Beech, and
the attractive Castle Inn
at Chiddingstone.
There is a restaurant and café at
Hever Castle, and the Village Tea
Rooms at Chiddingstone

A view of rolling countryside from the tower of Penshurst church

START & ROUTE DIRECTIONS

Start

Penshurst village lies between Sevenoaks and Tunbridge Wells, west of Tonbridge on the B2176. Park with care in the layby on the B2176 opposite Penshurst Place.

Directions

① ᚛ From the parking place, go to the centre of Penshurst and turn right along the B2188, signposted 'Tunbridge Wells'. In ½ mile (1km) turn right, signposted to Chiddingstone Hoath, and continue for ¼ mile (0.5km) to reach a T-junction. Turn right, towards Chidd Hoath, and in ½ mile (1km) bear left, signposted 'Markbeech/ Cowden'.

② ᚛ Continue, and in 1 mile (1.5km) bear left again towards Cowden. Pass through Horseshoe Green and go under the railway bridge. Cross the B2026 and enter the village of Cowden. Pass the church and take the first turning right. Follow the road away from the village, and pass Waystrode Manor. Continue for 1 mile (1.5km) and bear right to meet the B2026 again at the Queen's Arms pub.

③ ᚛ Continue straight ahead, signposted to

The village of Chiddingstone is a favourite period setting for films

Markbeech and Hever Castle. After 1 mile (1.5km), in Markbeech turn left into Uckfield Lane, by The Kentish Horse pub. Go down the hill, and after 1½ miles (2.5km) turn right opposite a bus shelter, signposted to Hever Castle and Penshurst, and continue into Hever village. Follow the road left, to pass Hever Castle on the right.

4 ⚄ Continue on this road, signposted 'Bough Beech'.

for 1½ miles (2.5km), meeting the railway line, and bear right to join the B2027 at The Wheatsheaf pub. Go straight on, and immediately after Chequers Garage, turn right. After 1 mile (1.5km) turn left at the crossroads into Chiddingstone village.

5 ⚄ Proceed through the village and in ½ mile (1km) take the right fork to pass through Weller's Town. After a further ½ mile (1km)

look out for a bridleway on the left by Lew Cross Farm. Turn left here and bear left again at Wat Stock, following the Eden Valley Walk back to the car park at Penshurst.
(*Alternatively*, go straight on at Lew Cross Farm to Hoath Corner. Turn left at The Rock pub, and continue, to meet the outward route at Chiddingstone Hoath. Turn left and left again following the signs to retrace the route to Penshurst.)

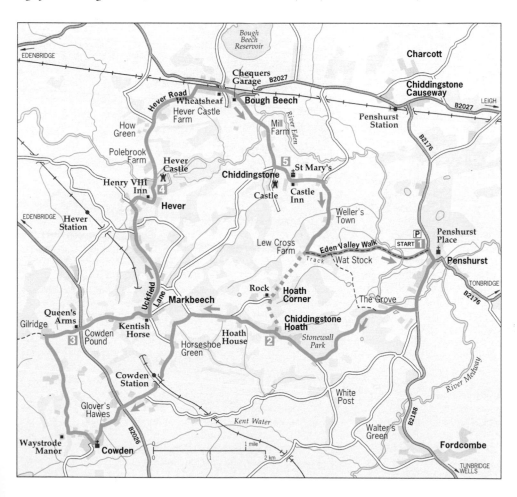

PLACES OF INTEREST

Penshurst: The village lies between the two rivers, Medway and Eden and has retained its character although overshadowed by the grandeur of Penshurst Place. Penshurst Place has been the home of the Sydney family since 1552. It fell into ruin and was restored by later generations of the family during the 19th century. The present incumbent, Lord de L'Isle, is a descendant of this family. The recently restored gardens date from the 14th century and the house can be visited. The church enclosed within the grounds is also of interest particularly for its entrance between some cottages.

Hever Castle: This moated 13th-century castle, with one of the finest castle gateways in England, is renowned for its connection with Anne Boleyn. In 1903 it was restored and beautifully furnished by the Astors, and is now a major tourist attraction and a conference centre. The adjoining Tudor 'village' is used as guest suites for conference delegates. The grounds have a 35 acre (14ha) lake, 30 acres (12ha) of gardens, including the unique Italian garden with a collection of Roman statues, and a maze (castle and gardens open from March to November).

Chiddingstone: Probably the most original village in Kent, Chiddingstone has retained its historic charm and has been used as a location for film settings. There are many examples of 16th- and 17th-

Gardens at Hever Castle

century architecture with half-timbered and tile-hung frontages to the houses. The most interesting of these is The Castle Inn, which dates from the 15th century or earlier. The village was acquired by the National Trust in 1939 except for the fine church of St Mary's. The Georgian Chiddingstone Castle is a remodelled 17th-century ironmaster's house (open from April to October). At the end of the village is the Chiding Stone, which is believed to have been a place where nagging wives were publicly 'chided'.

WHAT TO LOOK OUT FOR

The well-kept timber-framed and tile-hung houses give an air of prosperity to this part of Kent.
Azaleas and rhododendrons provide the colour in early summer and the many trees attract an abundance of woodland birds, including woodpeckers.
The route passes some unusual rock formations including the famous Chiding Stone in Chiddingstone.

Tenterden and the Weald of Kent

Apart from leaving and entering Tenterden, this is a route which is mainly on country lanes. It starts with a gentle climb to Sissinghurst, and then continues along the level roads of the Weald of Kent, passing through attractive villages in a landscape dominated by farmland – both arable and grazing – and with a stretch of forest.

RIDE 17
KENT
TQ883332

INFORMATION

Total Distance
24 miles (38.5km),
with 1 mile (1.5km) off-road

Grade
2

OS Maps
Landranger 1:50,000 sheets 188
(Maidstone & The Weald of Kent) and
189 (Ashford & Romney Marsh)

Tourist Information:
Tenterden, tel: 01580 763572

Cycle Shops/Hire
Apollo Cycle Sport, Tenterden,
(repairs), tel: 01580 765612;
Tiger Cycles, Tenterden (repairs
and hire),
tel: 01580 763838

Nearest Railway Station
Ashford (12 miles/19km)

Refreshments
There is a wealth of pubs and tea
rooms in Tenterden,
and good pubs along the route
include The Three Chimneys at
Biddenden (good garden), The Bell at
Smarden, and The George at
Bethersden; there is a restaurant and
café at Sissinghurst

Weather-boarding at Tenterden

Start

Tenterden lies between Ashford and Hastings on the A28. Park in Bridewell Lane, on the south side of the High Street (pay and display).

Directions

1 From the car park turn left into the High Street, and at the end of the town continue straight ahead on the A28, signposted 'Hastings'. Descend the hill, and after a short distance turn right onto a minor road, signposted 'Cranbrook'. Keep on this road for 6 miles (9.5km), passing straight over the crossroads at The Brogues and through Hemsted Forest, to reach the crossroads at Golford by the Tollgate Cottage. Turn right here and descend, before climbing the short hill up to a T-junction in Sissinghurst. Turn right on to the A262, signposted to Biddenden and Sissinghurst Gardens, and

The gateway at Sissinghurst leads through to the castle and beyond to the lovely gardens created by Vita Sackville-West

in ½ mile (1km) turn left into the drive leading to Sissinghurst Castle and Gardens.

2 Keep straight on to pass in front of the castle and garden entrance, and bear right after the buildings, with a stream and a white hexagonal summer house on the right. Ignore the marker and track to the right but keep straight ahead on a track, rising across a field, and meet the road by an iron gate. Bear right, and in ¼ mile (0.5km) fork left on to a minor country road, signposted 'Headcorn'.

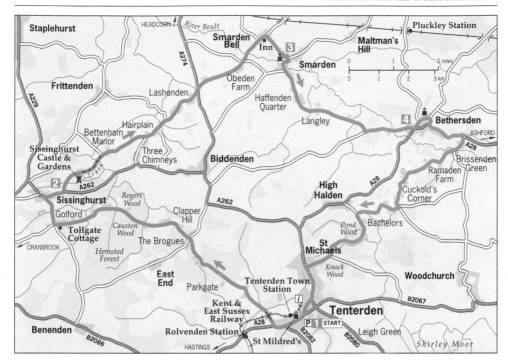

At the next T-junction, turn left and stay on this road for 3 miles (5km), passing through Lashenden and crossing the A274 to reach The Smarden Bell pub. Turn right shortly after the pub and follow this road to the village of Smarden.

3 ⚅ The entrance to the village is by a narrow Z-bend; immediately after this, bear right, with the church gate on the right. After ¼ mile (0.5km) to bear left at a fork, signposted to Bethersden. Stay on this road for 3 miles (5km), following signs to Bethersden, to meet the A28. Turn left and, as this is a busy road, turn immediately left again into Bethersden village.

4 ⚅ Follow the road which loops around the village to rejoin the A28 on the other side. Turn left and continue on the A28 for 1 mile (1.5km) before turning right into a minor road, signposted 'Woodchurch'. Take the first turning right in Brissenden Green, signposted 'High Halden'. Keep left by a converted oast house to finally meet a crossroads at Cuckold's Corner. Turn right, here, signposted to High Halden and Tenterden. After about 1 mile (1.5km) turn left, at a sharp curve in the road, into Harbourne Lane, signposted 'St Michaels'. Follow this winding road for 2 miles (3km) to reach the A28 in St Michaels. Turn left here to return to Tenterden and the car park in 1¼ miles (2km).

The church and houses at Smarden

PLACES OF INTEREST

Tenterden: This is a pleasant country town, still retaining much of its old character and individual shops. Many historic houses survive, and the church, St Mildred's, which dominates the town, is worth a visit. The prosperity of the town stems from 14th-century sheep farming and the Wealden cloth industry. This was further enhanced by the neighbouring shipbuilding industry at Smallhythe and Reading Street, when the surrounding areas were flooded. Today, the main tourist attraction is the Kent & East Sussex Railway, which is supported by enthusiasts of steam and diesel trains.

Sissinghurst Castle and Gardens: Although the castle is really the remains of a splendid Elizabethan mansion, the renowned gardens are the main attraction having been established by Vita Sackville-West in the 1930s. The restaurant in a converted barn provides a welcome ' refreshment break, with views over the surrounding countryside. The property is now owned by the National Trust. (Open from April to October, not Mondays; gardens may be very popular in summer.)

Tenterden is the headquarters of the Kent & East Sussex Railway

Smarden: This is one of the prettiest villages in Kent. The white-boarded cottages provide the character. The church of St Michael is so big and spacious inside that it has been nicknamed 'the barn of Kent', and the picturesque view of the church and enclosed churchyard from the north-east entrance is particularly impressive.

WHAT TO LOOK OUT FOR

The white painted weather boards make a perfect backdrop for the colourful cottage gardens in the summer. The oast houses, no longer used for their original purpose, still remain a typical feature of the Kent countryside, although many have been converted into stylish homes. Bethersden churchyard has some unusual burial vaults.

Hambleden and the South-west Chilterns

This ride through pleasant Chiltern villages and beechwoods uses undulating lanes with no off-road cycling. There is one severe climb after leaving Turville. While attractive all the year round, the area is especially beautiful in early autumn, when the beech trees are probably at their most colourful.

RIDE 18
BUCKINGHAMSHIRE
SU784865

INFORMATION

Total Distance
20 miles (32km), with diversion of
3½ miles (5.5km)

Grade
3

OS Maps
Landranger 1:50,000 sheet 175
(Reading & Windsor)

Tourist Information
Henley, tel: 01491 578034

Cycle Shop
Saddle Safari, Duke Street, Marlow,
tel: 01628 477020.
Nearest Railway Station: Henley
(5 miles/8km)

Refreshments
Good pubs along the route
include The Stag and Huntsman
at Hambleden, The Frog at Skirmett,
The Bull and Butcher at Turville,
The Fox and Hounds at
Christmas Common,
and The Five Horseshoes
at Maidensgrove.
There is a picnic area in
Cowleaze Wood

A curious two-legged sculpture, one of many to be encountered on the Sculpture Trail in Cowleaze Wood

START & ROUTE DIRECTIONS

Start

Hambleden is 2 miles (3km) north of Mill End which is itself situated midway between Henley and Marlow on the A4155. Start the ride from the free public car park in Hambleden village alongside The Stag and Huntsman pub. The car park is sign-posted from the village centre.

Directions

1. ⚲ Turn left downhill from the car park for 70yds (60m). Turn right with the church on your left and follow this lane to the crossroads at Pheasant's Hill. Turn right and then immediately left along Bottom Hill to the T-junction at Colstrope. Turn left down the hill and over the Hamble Brook to the junction with the Hambleden Valley road. Turn right and remain on

this undulating road through Skirmett for 2 miles (3km) to reach the outskirts of Fingest.

2. ⚲ Turn left, signed to Turville and Ibstone, at the top of the short hill just before Fingest church. Ignore the right turning up the hill to Ibstone, and instead continue to the staggered road junction. Bear slightly right to Turville. Stay on this lane through the village and up

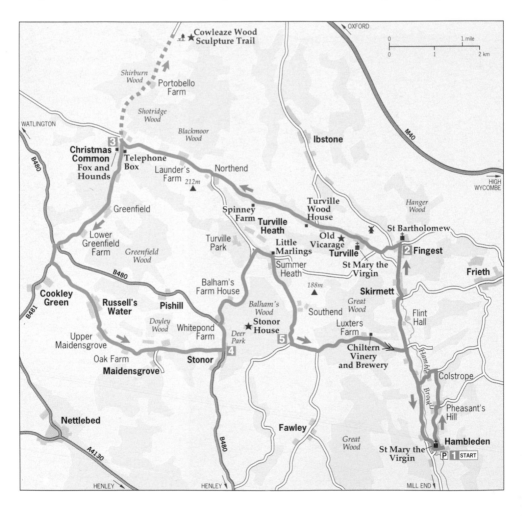

the valley, ignoring the right hand turning. Pass Turville Wood House on the left. Climb steeply through woodland, passing the entrance to Spinney Farm, to the T-junction near Northend. Turn right on a level road and continue for 1½ miles (2.5km) to Christmas Common. (At this point a diversion to the right right leads to the attrcative Cowleaze Wood picnic area and the Sculpture Trail.)

3 🚲 Bear sharply left at the junction to pass The Fox and Hounds pub on the right and a telephone box on the left. Stay on this road for 1¾ miles (3km) to the next crossroads, a junction of the B480 and the B481. Turn ,

right and then shortly left to join the B481, signed 'Nettlebed'. In 400yds (365m) turn off left down a single track road. Continue for 3 miles (5km), passing through Russell's Water and Maidensgrove, and descend through beechwoods to the T-junction with the B480 at Stonor.

4 🚲 Turn left with care and pass the entrance to Stonor Park and House. Turn right, signed to Turville Heath and Northend, and pass Whitepond Farm before climbing steadily up to Turville Heath. Fork right just before the Turville Heath

The flint-knapped church of St Mary at Hambleden

sign, and right again after 50yds (45m). Pass the entrance to Rose Farm House and shortly after, opposite Little Marlings, turn right. Continue on a level road for 1 mile (1.5km) through Southend to the next T-junction.

5 🚲 Turn left here, and soon, where the road bears sharply right, go straight ahead on the single track road. Proceed for 2 miles (3km) passing the Chiltern Vinery and Brewery before dropping steeply down (take care) to the T-junction. Turn right and continue for 1¼ miles (2km) to the outskirts of Hambleden; bear left return to the centre of the village and the car park.

PLACES OF INTEREST

Hambleden: The village, built around the Hamble Brook, has as its centre a pump complete with a chestnut tree.

The church of St Mary the Virgin has been much altered over the centuries. It contains a decorated chancel roof, and a carved wooden altar front which includes the coat of arms of Cardinal Wolsey and is thought to have originally been part of his bed-head.

The manor is situated in the village, and was the birthplace of Lord Cardigan, the leader of the Light Brigade.

Fingest: Dominating this pretty village is the Norman church of St Bartholomew. The tower is crowned by a saddle-back roof and its walls are almost 4ft (1m) thick.

Turville: Tiled and gabled cottages face one side of a small green, while opposite stands the church of St Mary the Virgin with its unusual squat tower. On a nearby hillside is a restored windmill which featured in the film *Chitty Chitty Bang Bang*. On the route out of the village is the Old Vicarage which has, on the roof, a miniature castellated tower.

Stonor: Stonor House, surrounded by a magnificent deer park, has been a family home for over 800 years. In the house can be seen painted and stained glass windows, fine furniture and sculptures. Stonor was a centre of Catholic resistance during their repression in the Elizabethan era. On view is the secret printing press which was in use during those times.

Sculpture Trail: The trail was opened in 1990 as a joint venture between the Forestry Commission and the Chiltern Sculpture Trust. The 17 exhibits are made from both natural and man-made products, and include one which consists of old drink cans and car mirrors.

WHAT TO LOOK OUT FOR

After winter the villages and cottage gardens are full of snowdrops and daffodils, while in late spring the beechwoods are ablaze with their new green foliage to be replaced later in the year by their rich autumn colours. Deer are often visible in the grounds of Stonor House. The Old Vicarage at Turville has, apart from its small tower on the roof, a notice on an outside wall indicating that the building was used as an air raid warden post in the last war.

The old mansion of Stonor

Windmills Around Thaxted

RIDE 19
ESSEX
TL612310

INFORMATION

Total Distance
18 miles (29km)

Grade
1

OS Maps
Landranger 1:50,000 sheets 167
(Chelmsford & Harlow)
and 154
(Cambridge & Newmarket)

Tourist Information
Saffron Walden, tel: 01799 510444

Cycle Shops/Hire
None on route

Nearest Railway Station
Elsenham (8 miles/13km)

Refreshments
Good range of pubs,
cafés and tea rooms in Thaxted,
Finchingfield and Great Bardfield
– in particular The Cake Table Tea
Shop in Thaxted,
and The Fox in Finchingfield.
Children are welcomed in
The Vine pub, and at the
Bardfield Centre Coffee Shop in
Great Bardfield

This is an easy all-road ride linking the picturesque villages of Thaxted, Finchingfield and Great Bardfield via gently rolling country lanes. Each village boasts a charming fully-restored windmill, historic buildings and interesting local museums.

The windmill at Thaxted was built in 1804, and now houses a museum

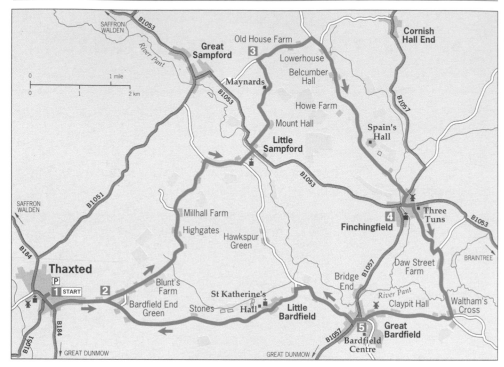

START & ROUTE DIRECTIONS

Start
The route starts at the historic market town of Thaxted, which is located on the B184 between Great Dunmow and Saffron Walden, 5 miles (8km) north of Great Dunmow. Park at the long stay car park (free) situated east of the High Street in Margarets Road.

Directions
1. 🚲 Turn left out of the car park, then turn right along Weaverthorpe Lane to a T-junction and bear right again to reach the High Street. Turn left along the B184, then after 200yds (185m) take the left turning, signposted 'The Bardfields'.

The church at Thaxted looms behind the ancient Guildhall

Gradually climb out of the village, bearing left at a fork of roads after ½ mile (1km) towards Little Sampford.

2. 🚲 Continue on this quiet narrow lane for 2 miles (3km) to a T-junction, and bear right for Little Sampford. In ½ mile (1km), turn left in front of Little Sampford church and descend to a T-junction with the B1053. Turn left, then immediately right on to a lane beside a thatched cottage. Proceed gently uphill and keep to this peaceful lane for over a mile, passing a fine moated farmhouse on the left, to an unsigned T-junction.

3. 🚲 Turn right, then on reaching a further T-junction turn right towards Finchingfield. Pass the lane for Cornish Hall End and continue for 2 miles (3km) on this rolling lane, passing the magnificent Spain's Hall on your left, before descending

into the charming village of Finchingfield. At a T-junction turn right and pass the wind-mill to reach the village centre.

4 🚲 Bear left uphill at the village green, pass the church on your right, then turn right by The Three Tuns pub into Vicarage Road. Shortly, leave the village on this narrow lane and in ½ mile (1km), keep right at a T-junction to pass Daw Street Farm. Descend to a bridge over the River Pant and climb steadily into Waltham's Cross. At a crossroads turn right, signed 'Great Bardfield' and remain on this lane for a mile, passing the green and windmill, to reach a T-junction in the village centre.

The village pond, Finchingfield

Neat cottages huddle close, near Thaxted windmill

5 🚲 You can turn left here for the Bardfield Centre (refreshments), or turn right uphill through the village, keeping left along the B1057, signed 'Great Dunmow'. In a

short distance turn right beside a timbered cottage, signposted to Thaxted. Remain on this undulating road through Little Bardfield and after 4 miles (6.5km) reach the B184 in Thaxted and retrace the outward route back to the car park.

WHAT TO LOOK OUT FOR

The prosperity of this part of East Anglia in medieval times resulted in wealthy farmers and merchants building grand country hall houses for themselves. Many were moated to keep intruders out or purely for status reasons, and a fine example – Maynards – can be seen between Little Sampford and Finchingfield (no public access).

Close to Finchingfield, note Spain's Hall, a splendid Tudor brick mansion. At Little Bardfield there is a well restored 16th-century hall situated beside the quaint church of St Katherine's, which has a Saxon tower. The church organ was built in 1688 for Jesus College in Cambridge.

PLACES OF INTEREST

Thaxted: Established in the 14th century, Thaxted rapidly became a flourishing market town due to the presence of a cutlery industry, and many well preserved old houses survive as a reminder that this was once a very prosperous place. The 15th-century church soars cathedral-like above the main street and was clearly built by a wealthy community. Below it, the magnificent timbered and jettied Guildhall dates from 1390 and incorporates an earlier ancient lockup. Along the street is The Manse, former home of the composer Gustav Holst, who resided in the town from 1915–25. Quaint cobbled streets lead up to 15th-century almshouses, beyond which lies John Webb's Windmill. Built in 1804, it commands fine views over the surrounding countryside and houses a fascinating rural museum.

The splendid façade of Spain's Hall

Finchingfield: Possibly the most photographed village in Essex, Finchingfield is a picture-book settlement complete with a church on a hill, a picturesque postmill, a hump-backed bridge and a village green with a duckpond surrounded by quaint cottages. Just below the church lies the 15th-century Guildhall which houses a small local museum and exhibitions in the old school room.

Great Bardfield: A major feature of this old market town is a restored windmill that stands on a green overlooking the pleasant mixture of colour-washed old cottages and pargetted houses. The small 16th-century Cottage Museum stands on the Dunmow Road and contains a collection of 19th- and 20th-century domestic and agricultural artefacts and some rural crafts. It is open on weekend and bank holiday afternoons in summer. The Bardfield Cage, a 19th-century village lockup is also open.

Lavenham and the Suffolk Wool Villages

This ride along quiet roads explores the gently rolling countryside and picturesque villages around the magnificent medieval wool town of Lavenham. Narrow traffic-free lanes wind around the Brett Valley, passing classic Suffolk hall houses, a small medieval chapel and the charming unspoilt settlements of Brent Eleigh, Chelsworth and Kersey.

RIDE 20
SUFFOLK
TL914489

INFORMATION

Distance
23 miles (37km)

Grade
2

OS Map
Landranger 1:50,000 sheet 155
(Bury St Edmunds & Sudbury)

Tourist Information
Lavenham (summer only),
tel: 01787 248207;
Bury St Edmunds,
tel: 01284 764667

Cycle Shops/Hire
None on the route

Nearest Railway Station
Sudbury (6 miles/10km)

Refreshments
Several excellent pubs,
tea rooms and restaurants, including
The Angel and The Swan,
in Lavenham.
On the route,
families are welcomed at
The Peacock Inn, Chelsworth and
The Bell at Kersey
(also teas in summer)

Herringbone brickwork between the timbers at Brent Eleigh

START & ROUTE DIRECTIONS

Start

Lavenham is situated on the A1141 between Hadleigh and Bury St Edmunds. Park at the car park (free) on Church Street beside The Cock Inn, opposite the parish church.

Directions

1 ᗕ Turn right out of the car park and head down the main street, which is lined with impressive buildings. Pass The Swan Inn, then bear off right along Market Street into the square. Continue past The Angel Inn, downhill to a T-junction. Turn left, then shortly bear right at a crossroads, signposted to Preston. Follow the lane right, then in 1 mile (1.5km)

turn right into Preston St Mary. Continue past the church and Preston Hall on your left, and soon bear right along Whelp Street, signed 'Brent Eleigh'.

2 ᗕ Gently climb and follow the narrow lane across farmland, with good views of the countryside, and descend into Brent Eleigh. Cross a bridge and bear left at a junction along the village lane (dead end). At the end, just beyond Street Farm, go through the gap in the fence and cross the A1141 with great care to join a lane, signed 'Milden'. Proceed across staggered crossroads at the B1115 and continue into Milden. Turn left before the

The bridge at Chelsworth

telephone box, pass Milden church and continue to a T-junction in Swingleton Green.

3 ᗕ Turn right and follow the valley lane for ½ mile (1km) to a further junction. Bear left, then almost immediately turn left along the A1141 for 150yds (135m). Where the main road bends sharply left, turn right on to the B1115 towards Bildeston. Pass through picturesque Chelsworth, turn right opposite The Peacock Inn and cross the narrow bridge over the River Brett. Climb to and cross the A1141 and shortly enter Lindsey Tye. Just beyond The Red Rose pub, turn left along a metalled by-way and continue for 1 mile (1.5km) to an unsigned T-junction. Turn right, and follow an undul-

ating lane to a T-junction, and turn right there for Kersey.

④ 🚲 The main route turns right at the village edge, signposted to the small medieval St James Chapel. Keep on this level lane for 4 miles (6.5km), passing the chapel on your left, keep straight on past The White Rose Inn, and disregard two lanes off to the left. Just beyond The Grove, turn right (unsigned) into the hamlet of Priory Green.

⑤ 🚲 Bear left through the hamlet and take the next turning right, signed 'Little Waldingfield', to reach the B1115 in the village centre

after about a mile. Turn right and bear left in 1 mile (1.5km), signposted to Sudbury. Follow this narrow meandering lane to the B1071 and turn right. Continue towards the

The Guildhall, Lavenham

prominent tower of Lavenham church, and reach the start point after 1 mile (1.5km).

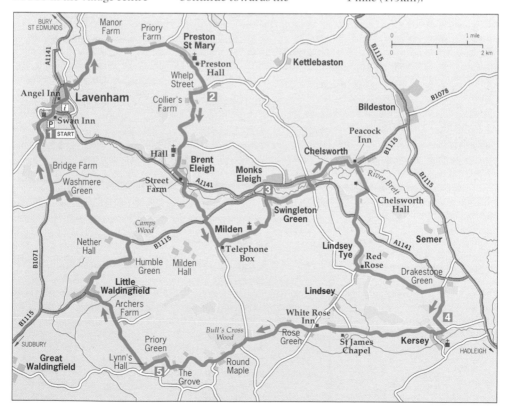

PLACES OF INTEREST

Lavenham: Often regarded as the finest medieval town in England, Lavenham has hardly changed appearance since its heyday as an important wool town in the 14th and 15th centuries. No less than 300 of its buildings are listed as being of architectural or historic interest, including immaculately preserved timber-framed houses such as the splendid 16th-century Guildhall (NT). It overlooks the market place and contains an exhibition of local history and the woollen cloth industry.

Other fine buildings to view are the medieval Priory, the 14th-century, timbered Little Hall, and the magnificent church of St Peter and St Paul with its 141ft (43m) tower.

Brent Eleigh: A picturesque group of thatched houses, with a row of almshouses dating from 1731, and a 14th-century church containing Jacobean woodwork and some fine wall paintings. The adjacent hall (not open) is Elizabethan, with modern additions by architect Sir Edward Lutyens.

Chelsworth: An attractive double hump-backed bridge spans the River Brett in this pretty village, which comprises a row of charming houses lining the north side of the village street and facing the parkland of Chelsworth Hall.

Kersey: This idyllic village is deservedly one of the beauty spots of Suffolk. Nestling in

Passing through the ford, Kersey

the Brett Valley, the single sloping street of this once-noted weaving centre leads down to a shallow ford, and is lined with a fascinating range of buildings from small weavers' cottages to large half-timbered merchants' houses and medieval pubs.

Impressively perched at the head of the village is the church, a gem of 14th- and 15th-century architecture, on a site mentioned in the Domesday Book.

WHAT TO LOOK OUT FOR

The countryside around Lavenham is sprinkled with timber-framed buildings and elegant colour-washed farmhouses or old hall houses. The presence of these in such numbers reflects the wealth of the farming communities here in medieval times. The Ordnance Survey map of the area reveals a surprising number of these buildings that were once or are still moated. Moats kept out unwanted visitors, provided daub for infilling of walls and acted as a source of water. Larger moats were built by the wealthier merchants as an indication of their own importance.

Blickling Hall and The Marriott Way

A fairly level and easy-going ride, this route begins at the splendid National Trust property of Blickling Hall, and incorporates a variety of parkland tracks, peaceful country lanes and a section of well surfaced disused railway track, The Marriott Way. Diversions along the route include a rose garden, a timeless estate village and fascinating churches.

RIDE 21
NORFOLK
TG175285

INFORMATION

Total Distance
21 miles (33.5km),
with 6 miles (9.5km) off-road

Grade
2

OS Map
Landranger 1:50,000 sheet 133
(North East Norfolk)

Tourist Information
Aylsham (summer only),
tel: 01263 733903; Norwich,
tel: 01603 666071

Cycle Hire
Reepham Station Museum of Shops
(summer), tel: 01603 871187

Nearest Railway Station
Aylsham. Bure Valley Railway links
with main line at Hoveton and
Wroxham for Norwich

Refreshments
Pub and good tea room with family
facilities at Blickling Hall; Mill
Restaurant at Itteringham and Rose
Tea Room at Mannington Hall
Gardens; The Earl Arms pub at
Heydon, Reepham and Aylsham
(also cafés). Excellent picnic spots
in Blickling Park

Cyclists on The Marriott Way

START & ROUTE DIRECTIONS

Start

The ride starts from the National Trust car park (free) at Blickling Hall, which is located on the B1354, 1½ miles (2.5km) north-west of Aylsham and 15 miles (24km) north of Norwich.

Directions

1 ⚲ From the car park follow the path to the information board and sign stating 'Park Only'. Turn left along the estate road, bearing right at a fork by some cottages to enter Blickling Park. After a short distance take the waymarked bridleway diagonally left across the park (Weavers' Way). Proceed for 1 mile (1.5km), passing a track to the Mausoleum, and keeping to the left of Great Wood to reach a parking area and lane.

2 ⚲ Turn left, then bear right at the next junction along the Bure Valley to a further junction by The Walpole Arms and the Mill Restaurant. Keep right, cross the river and pass through Itteringham, following signs to Mannington. After ½ mile (1km) turn left towards Corpusty and shortly pass Mannington Hall on your right and the entrance to the gardens. Continue, and at a T-junction turn left along a gently undulating lane. Stay on this for 1½ miles (2.5km) to the junction of the B1354 and B1149.

3 ⚲ Continue straight on into Saxthorpe. Cross the

An unusual sculpture of horseshoes at Heydon Park

River Bure and turn right in front of the shop, signed 'Little London'. Almost immediately turn left by The Dukes Head pub to climb out of the village. The views are good; stay on this lane for 1½ miles (2.5km), passing Cropton Hall, to reach a T-junction. Turn left, then at a crossroads bear left again into the attractive and unspoilt estate village of Heydon.

4 ⚲ Return to the crossroads and proceed straight over, signposted to Salle. In about a mile keep right at a junction around Salle Park, then take the next lane right towards Salle Church. Continue through the hamlet, turn left at a T-junction towards Reepham, and proceed for 1 mile (1.5km) to the B1145 on the edge of the village.

5 🚲 Keep straight ahead towards Reepham, then in a few yards turn left, opposite the old railway bridge, and pass through a gate to join The Marriott Way – a good, surfaced cycling trail along the former railway track. In 2 miles (3km) pass under a bridge and immediately fork left to climb on to an embankment (the former platform of Cawston Station). Continue to a level crossing and cross a by-road.

The lofty interior of Salle Church

6 🚲 Proceed for a further 4 miles (6.5km) through open country to the end of the trail, at a gate adjoining the B1354 in Aylsham. Turn left through the town centre, remaining on the B-road and in ½ mile (1km) fork left on to an unclassified lane. In 1 mile (1.5km) at Abel Heath (NT), fork right and pass through the hamlet of Silvergate to reach the B1354, opposite Blickling church. Turn left to return to the National Trust car park and start point.

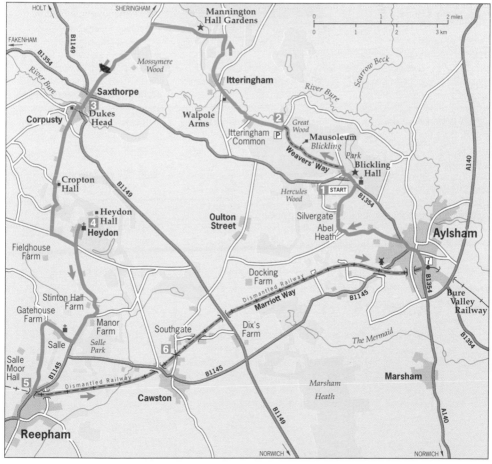

PLACES OF INTEREST

Looking across to Salle Church

Blickling Hall: Flanked by 17ft (5m), dark yew hedges planted in the 17th century, this magnificent Jacobean brick-fronted hall is one of the great houses of East Anglia. Dutch gabling, mullioned windows and domed turrets characterise the exterior. Inside there are fine collections of furniture, pictures and tapestries, and a spectacular Jacobean plaster ceiling in the 123ft (37.5m) Long Gallery (moulded in the 1620s) is very impressive. The gardens are also well worth exploring. (Open from April to October but not Mondays or Thursdays, except Bank Holidays.)

Mannington Hall Gardens: Outstanding gardens surround a moated medieval manor house (not open). There are walled herbaceous borders, a scented garden, and a noted rose collection featuring old-fashioned varieties is set in an acre of walled kitchen garden. Wild flowers abound around the ruins of a Saxon church and Victorian follies. (The gardens are open on selected summer days, the park all year round.)

Heydon: This is a most attractive estate village, built around a charming green where time seems to have stood still, at the end of a dead-end lane. Heydon Hall (open by appointment only) dates from 1581 and has an E-shaped front. The grounds include an ice-house and a lookout tower.

Salle Church: The tiny village of Salle is the unlikely setting for a 15th-century cathedral-like church full of rich treasures, apparently totally out of proportion to the tiny parish it serves. It was built by three wealthy families: the Briggs, the Fontaynes and the Boleyns. Of particular note is the unusual font, one of the seven-sacrament fonts, of which 39 are said to exist.

Aylsham: An old market town on the River Bure, Aylsham has many attractive Georgian houses. The famous landscape gardener Humphrey Repton (1752–1818) is buried in the churchyard, with the epitaph he composed himself.

WHAT TO LOOK OUT FOR

Both the churches at Heydon and Salle hide notable features. Remarkable 14th-century wall paintings, first disclosed in 1970, grace the walls in Heydon church, and the splendid painted rood screen dates from 1480. Well worth finding in Salle church are the 26 carved oak stalls. Some have good carvings of human heads, others boast birds and animals; note the swan, squirrel, dragon and ape. Look out, too, for the strange horse sculptures created from horseshoes in Heydon.

RIDE 22
NORFOLK
TF832422

The Burnhams and Holkham Park

This ride offers an excellent day's cycling, exploring the delights of rural North Norfolk. Beginning at the charming little town of Burnham Market, the ride incorporates the magnificent deer park that surrounds Holkham Hall, a glorious sandy beach, the pilgrimage village of Little Walsingham, and Burnham Thorpe, notable as the birthplace of Lord Nelson.

INFORMATION

Distance
28 miles (45km), with 5 miles (8km) on parkland drives

Grade
2

OS Map
Landranger 1:50,000 sheet 132 (North West Norfolk)

Tourist Information
Little Walsingham (summer only), tel: 01328 820510;
Hunstanton, tel: 01485 532610

Cycle Hire
Dial House Information Barn (NT), Brancaster Staithe (summer), tel: 01485 210719;
Bircham Windmill Cycle Hire, Great Bircham, tel: 01485 578393

Nearest Railway Station
King's Lynn (20 miles/32km)

Refreshments
The splendid Hoste Arms in Burnham Market offers lunches and teas; there is a tea room at Holkham Hall (and excellent picnic spots throughout the Park and at Holkham Beach);
pubs and cafés in Walsingham, teas at the Slipper Chapel and in North Creake;
a warm family welcome at the unspoilt Lord Nelson pub in Burnham Thorpe

Abbey ruins, Little Walsingham

START & ROUTE DIRECTIONS

Start:
Burnham Market is located at the junction of the B1155 and the B1355, just off the A149 coast road between Hunstanton and Cromer, 5 miles (8km) west of Wells-Next-The-Sea. Park carefully along the main street, near the green.

Directions
1 🚲 Head east away from the church, keeping left through the town along the B1155 towards Wells-Next-The-Sea. Turn right through Burnham Overy Town with its mills over the River Burn, and after 1 mile (1.5km) bear right into Holkham Park, signed 'Garden Centre'. Pass the walled Garden Centre, and at the end of the lake keep left, soon to bear right on the estate road that runs in front of the Hall. At a junction turn left (private ahead) and shortly leave the park via gates. Continue through the estate village to the A149 (tea rooms and gallery in Holkham to the right), and cross straight over the main road to follow the access road to the magnificent sandy beach.

2 🚲 Retrace your steps back into the Park, to the fork of estate roads beyond the Hall, near the lake. Bear left and proceed through the deer park. Pass the obelisk and gently ascend to gates on the perimeter. Turn left along a lane, go over a crossroads and continue to a further crossroads. Keep straight

on, signed 'Wighton', and follow this narrow lane, with good views out to sea, for 2 miles (3km) to reach the B1105 at Wighton.

3 🚲 Turn right, then immediately bear off left along the village street, signed 'Binham'. Pass All Saints Church and the Sandpiper Inn, then cross the River Stiffkey and shortly bear off right for Great Walsingham. After 1 mile (1.5km) reach the B1388 in the village, turn right, then right again signposted 'Unbridged Ford'. Cross the footbridge over the stream,

bear left by the memorial cross into St Peters Road and shortly pass the parish church before joining the B1105 on the edge of Little Walsingham.

4 🚲 Turn left into the village centre. Keep left, then turn right at a T-junction, and follow the B1105 through the High Street. Leave the village and after ¼ mile (0.5km) bear off right towards Barsham. Follow this level lane parallel to the River Stiffkey and soon reach the Slipper Chapel. Continue to the hamlet of North Barsham, bear right by the green and gradually climb

An old timber-framed house in Little Walsingham

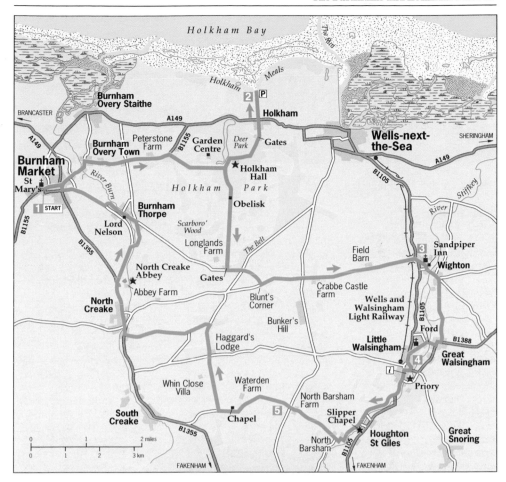

out of the valley on a tiny lane to a crossroads.

5 🚲 Go straight over, signposted 'Waterden', pass a chapel on your right, and then turn right for North Holkham. After about a mile go over a crossroads and proceed on a lane through woodland, then take the next lane left, signed 'The Creakes'. Where the lane curves left, keep straight ahead (unsigned) and descend into North Creake and the B1355. Turn right, and after nearly a

mile bear right for Burnham Thorpe. (To visit the ruins of North Creake Abbey follow the driveway towards Abbey Farm.) In ½ mile (1km) bear right over the River Burn and soon turn left at a crossroads to pass through Burnham Thorpe. On reaching a T-junction, turn right, then after ¾ mile (1km) turn right into Burnham Market and keep left at The Lord Nelson pub for the village centre.

Burnham Market is the largest of the seven 'Burnhams'

PLACES OF INTEREST

Burnham Market: The largest of seven 'Burnhams' that cluster together along this fine stretch of coastline, this is a handsome little town with a wide green, a small stream flowing across the main road and a collection of fine Georgian houses near the green and St Mary's Church.

Holkham Hall: This vast Palladian mansion is one of Britain's most majestic stately homes, situated in lake-watered parkland laid out by 'Capability' Brown in 1762. The house dates from the 18th century and contains a superb hall by William Kent, splendidly appointed state apartments with an impressive art collection and fine furnishings. A Bygones Museum houses an evocative collection of over 4,000 domestic and agricultural artefacts. (Open on summer afternoons only, Sunday to Thursday.)

Little Walsingham: The village is noted for its medieval history and architecture, and as a place of pilgrimage since 1061. Remains of the Augustinian Priory, the original site of the Shrine of Our Lady, can be seen in the grounds of the new abbey. Virtually every English king from Richard I to Henry VIII journeyed to the famous shrine. Ancient timber-framed houses line the Common Place, and the Shirehall Museum displays the history of the village. The 10¼ inch gauge Wells and Walsingham Light Railway is the longest of its kind in the world, and passes through some fine scenery (summer only).

Slipper Chapel: Built in 1325 as the last wayside chapel for pilgrims before Walsingham, it was here that the pilgrims took off their shoes and walked the Holy Mile into the village.

The magnificent Holkham Hall

North Creake Abbey: Originally a hospital and almshouse for the poor, it later gained Abbey status. Dissolved in 1506 due to the sudden death by plague of all its inmates, its remains include the 13th-century presbytery and transepts.

Burnham Thorpe: This peaceful little village beside the River Burn was the birthplace in 1758 of Lord Nelson. The font in which he was christened is in the 13th-century parish church, alongside a lectern and rood made from the timbers of HMS *Victory*.

WHAT TO LOOK OUT FOR

The fine parkland of Holkham Hall is home to a herd of fallow deer, and Egyptian and Canada geese can be seen on the lake. The plantation of Corsican pines that fronts Holkham Beach is a haven for goldcrests and occasionally crossbills. The neighbouring fields and marshes are feeding grounds for oystercatchers, curlew and lapwings, and in winter flocks of geese are regular visitors. This stretch of coastline is a birdwatcher's paradise.
In early summer the quiet lanes are lined with bright yellow fields of oilseed rape fringed with poppies.
Look out for the sign on nearing Burnham Thorpe directing you to the plaque in the wall, which points out that Nelson was born in the rectory that once stood beyond the wall; it was pulled down in 1803.

Chipping Campden and the Northern Cotswolds

RIDE 23
GLOUCESTERSHIRE
SP150390

This route takes you on a fairly short, undulating ride through picturesque rolling countryside around the beautiful market town of Chipping Campden. Honey-coloured stone hamlets and villages are linked by scenic lanes, affording excellent views, and garden admirers have the opportunity to visit two of England's most delightful gardens – Hidcote Manor and Kiftsgate.

INFORMATION

Total Distance
18 miles (29km)

Grade
2

OS Map
Landranger 1:50,000 sheet 151
(Stratford-upon-Avon).

Tourist Information
Stow-on-the-Wold, tel: 01451 831082

Cycle Hire
Cotswold Country Cycles, Longlands
Farm Cottage, Hidcote Boyce (on the
ride), tel: 01386 438706;
Jeffrey Toyshop, Moreton-in-Marsh,
tel: 01608 650756

Nearest Railway Station
Honeybourne (5 miles/8km);
Moreton-in-Marsh (7 miles/11.5km)

Refreshments
Excellent choice of
tea rooms, pubs and hotels in
Chipping Campden;

summer teas at
Longlands Farm Cottage, Hidcote
Boyce;
both Hidcote Manor and Kiftsgate
Gardens offer refreshments in
summer;
tea rooms in Blockley;
families are welcome at The Ebrington
Arms, Ebrington, in The Crown at
Blockley, and especially at
The Bakers Arms in Broad Campden
(special menu and play area)
along the way

*Mellow stonework at the
Batsford Stud*

START & ROUTE DIRECTIONS

Start

Chipping Campden is situated on the B4081, 2½ miles (4km) north of the A44 Evesham to Stow-on-the-Wold road, 7 miles (11.5km) north of Stow. Parking is available along the main street and in a couple of small car parks; may be busy in summer.

Directions

1️⃣ 🚲 Head north along the B4081 (High Street) out of the town centre. After ¾ mile (1km) bear right with the B4081, signed to Stratford-upon-Avon. Shortly, turn right on to an unclassified lane towards Hidcote Boyce and follow the

undulating lane past Longlands Farm (summer teas) to a crossroads, near the top of a steady climb. Turn left and continue, with far-reaching views across the vale of Evesham to the Malvern Hills, to reach the entrance to Kiftsgate Court Garden, and the access road to Hidcote Bartrim and Hidcote Manor Gardens.

2️⃣ 🚲 Retrace the route back past Hidcote House, and take the next turning left into Hidcote Boyce. Bear right through the hamlet and take the first turning on the right to reach the crossroads encountered earlier. Turn left, signed 'Ebrington', and keep on this gently

A converted silk mill, Blockley

Almshouses stand near St James's Church, Chipping Campden

undulating lane with rolling Cotswolds views to reach a junction in Ebrington. Turn left, then shortly bear right

beside the green and memorial cross, signposted 'Paxford', and pass The Ebrington Arms.

③ ᧿ Descend on a narrow lane, and keep straight on across the B4035. In ½ mile (1km) turn right at a T-junction on to the B4479 and enter Paxford. Soon bear left towards Aston Magna, then keep left (unsigned) by the green (The Churchill Arms is straight ahead). Continue with care along a narrow pitted lane for 2 miles (3km) into Aston Magna.

④ ᧿ Turn right opposite the church (now a private house), climb uphill over the railway and turn left, signposted to Batsford. Ascend with views across Moreton-in-Marsh, and proceed for about a mile to a junction where the road bears sharp left. Go straight ahead, signed 'Village Only' to visit the estate village of Batsford. (To visit the Arboretum and Falconry Centre in Batsford Park, extend the ride into Moreton-in-Marsh, joining the A44 towards Bourton-on-the-Hill to reach the access driveway – a return trip of 6 miles (10km).

⑤ ᧿ Return along the ridge road for ½ mile (1km) and turn left for Blockley. Descend the steep hill into Draycott, following the lane sharp left to reach the B4479 after 1 mile (1.5km). Turn left into Blockley, and shortly turn right, signposted to the village centre. At a T-junction, turn left to explore the village;

otherwise, head right towards Broad Campden.

⑥ ᧿ Keep to this scenic, lane beside Northwick Park and in 1 mile (1.5km) descend into Broad Campden. Turn left to pass through the village, and proceed for 1 mile (1.5km) to the B4081. Turn right for the short ride back into the centre of Chipping Campden.

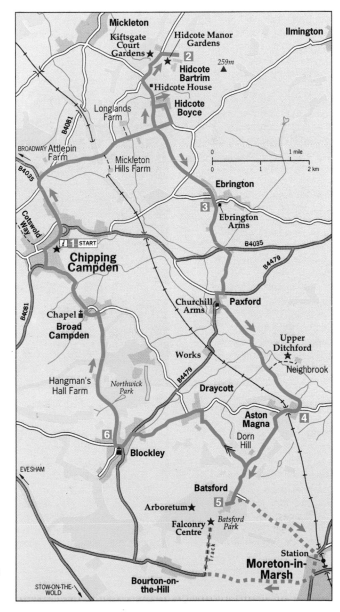

PLACES OF INTEREST

Chipping Campden: The glow of golden limestone is everywhere in this beautiful, unspoiled Cotswold market town. In the High Street don't miss the fine 17th-century gabled Market Hall (NT), the 14th-century Woolstaplers Hall and the splendid row of almshouses leading to the 15th-century church of St James, one of the finest Cotswold 'wool' churches. Wool made the town prosperous and a large memorial brass in the church is dedicated to William Grevel, 'the flower of the wool merchants of all England'.

Gardens: Two splendid and very popular formal gardens are encountered on this ride, both open on selected days in the summer. At Kiftsgate the chief attraction is the collection of old-fashioned roses. These include the largest rose in England, the *Rosa felipes* 'Kiftsgate'. Hidcote Manor Garden (NT) is one of the most delightful in the country, created this century by the horticulturist Major Lawrence Johnston. It comprises a series of small gardens, separated by walls and hedges of different species, and is notable for rare shrubs, 'old' roses and interesting plant species.

Batsford: This charming little estate village is on the edge of Batsford Park, which boasts one of the largest collections of trees in Great Britain in its 50-acre (20ha) Arboretum. There are well over a thousand different species of tree, including numerous varieties of maple and magnolia.

Blockley: An unusually large village for its remote location, Blockley's size is due to its once prosperous silk industry – in 1884, six mills employed 600 people. It is an attractive place, and the fine manor of nearby Northwick Park and the large Norman church are evidence of Blockley's former stature.

Broad Campden: Features of this peaceful village include an 18th-century Friends' Meeting House that has been restored, and a much older Chapel House – a 12th-century chapel converted into a private dwelling.

Part of the beautiful formal garden at Kiftsgate

WHAT TO LOOK OUT FOR

In Chipping Campden note the distinctive gatehouses near the church. These are the only surviving remains of one of the great lost mansions of the Cotswolds, Campden House, which was destroyed during the Civil War.
Locate the old shop in Paxford to view the traditional Hovis and Spillers dog food advertising signs on its stone façade.
From the lane between Paxford and Aston Magna (along the private drive to Neighbrook), look out for the field impressions of the lost medieval village of Upper Ditchford, one of an estimated 165 'lost villages' in Gloucestershire.

On the Trail of William Shakespeare

RIDE 24
WARWICKSHIRE
SP196540

INFORMATION

Total Distance
19 miles (31km),
with 2½ miles (4km) off-road

Grade
2

OS Maps
Landranger 1:50,000 sheets 151
(Stratford-upon-Avon) and 150
(Worcester & The Malverns)

Tourist Information
Stratford-upon-Avon,
tel: 01789 293127

Cycle Shops/Hire
Clarkes (hire/repairs), Stratford-upon-

Beginning from Stratford-upon-Avon, the birthplace of the celebrated Elizabethan poet and playwright William Shakespeare, this relatively gentle ride explores the Avon Valley and some of the villages and properties associated with the great literary figure. It includes a few short climbs and a delightful stretch of old railway track – The Greenway.

Avon, tel: 01789 205057; Knotts Cycles, Stratford-upon-Avon, tel: 01789 205149; Pashleys Cycle Store, Stratford-upon-Avon, tel: 01789 292263

Nearest Railway Station
Stratford-upon-Avon

Refreshments
Plenty of cafés and pubs in Stratford; pubs along the route at Welford-on-Avon, Aston Cantlow and Wilmcote,

and children are welcome at The Blue Boar, Temple Grafton;. tea room at Home Farm Stores in Aston Cantlow, and afternoon teas are served at The Swan House Inn, Wilmcote; both Anne Hathaway's Cottage and Mary Arden's House offer refreshments. Good picnic areas along The Greenway beside the River Avon and at Milcote

Anne Hathaway's Cottage is almost hidden beneath its low thatched roof

Ancient bike, Mary Arden's House

START & ROUTE DIRECTIONS

Start

Park in the free car park at the beginning of The Greenway, located at a roundabout on the A4390, ½ mile (1km) south of Stratford-upon-Avon town centre. *Note:* if carrying bikes on the roof of the car, beware of the height restriction barrier at the car park entrance.

Directions

⬛1⬛ ⛭ From the car park join The Greenway, the well-surfaced cycle/walking track that follows the course of the old railway through the Avon Valley. After 2½ miles (4km) reach Milcote car park and picnic area and turn right along a lane. Shortly, keep right, signed 'Weston' and 'Welford', and in ¾ mile (1km) turn right to visit the attractive hamlet of Weston-on-Avon.

⬛2⬛ ⛭ Return to the lane, turn right and continue to a T-junction. Turn right into Welford-on-Avon, and bear left at The Bell pub to visit the church. Proceed through the village and cross the River Avon to reach the B439. Turn right and shortly afterwards left, signposted 'Binton'. Gently ascend out of the valley, pass through Binton, and at a crossroads by The Blue Boar pub, turn left towards Temple Grafton.

⬛3⬛ ⛭ Follow the undulating lane into the village, and beyond the church turn right, signed 'Haselor'. Continue for 1 mile (1.5km) and cross over the busy A46 with care. Go through the hamlet of Haselor, turn right at a crossroads and shortly enter the picturesque village of Walcote. Bear left out of the village, and at a further crossroads, keep straight ahead into Mill Lane, signed to Aston Cantlow. After about a mile, turn left into Brook Road to explore Aston Cantlow.

⬛4⬛ ⛭ Return along the lane, following it sharp left to pass a house called Teapot Hall, then in ¾ mile (1km) turn left for Wilmcote. Proceed uphill into the village centre and turn left opposite The Swan House Inn to visit Mary Arden's House. Continue along the village street, and in 1 mile (1.5km) turn left, signed 'Stratford', and proceed for 1½ miles (2.5km), crossing over the A46, to reach the A422 and the edge of Stratford.

⬛5⬛ ⛭ Turn left, and after about ½ mile (1km) turn right into Church Lane for Shottery. On reaching a mini-roundabout, bear right to visit Anne Hathaway's Cottage. Return to the roundabout and follow signs for the town centre through the village. Continue to a roundabout at the junction with the B439 and A4390 and go straight over into Seven Meadows Lane, signed 'Broadway' (cycle lane on the opposite side of the road). Shortly, reach a second roundabout, to return to the car park.

Shakespeare's Birthplace, Stratford

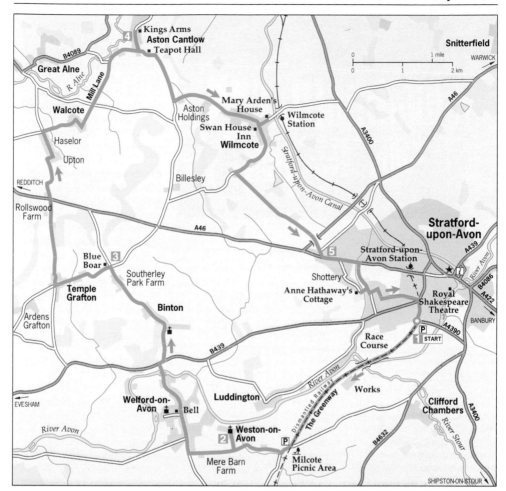

Kings Arms
Aston Cantlow
Teapot Hall
4
Snitterfield
WARWICK
B4089
Great Alne
R. Alne
Mill Lane
A46
Walcote
Aston
Holdings
Mary Arden's
House
Wilmcote
Station
Haselor
Swan House
Inn
Wilmcote
REDDITCH
Upton
Billesley
Stratford-upon-Avon Canal
A3400
Rollswood
Farm
A46
Stratford-
upon-Avon
A439
Blue
Boar
3
5
Stratford-upon-
Avon Station
River Avon
B4086
Temple
Grafton
Southerley
Park Farm
Shottery
Royal
Shakespeare
Theatre
A422
Ardens
Grafton
Binton
Anne Hathaway's
Cottage
BANBURY
B439
Race
Course
P
1 START
A4390
EVESHAM
River Avon
The Greenway
Works
Dismantled Railway
Clifford
Chambers
A3400
Welford-on-
Avon
Bell
Luddington
River Avon
River Stour
Mere Barn
Farm
2
Weston-on-
Avon
P
Milcote
Picnic Area
B4632
SHIPSTON-ON-STOUR

1 mile
1
2 km

A venerable timbered house at Aston Cantlow

PLACES OF INTEREST

Stratford-upon-Avon: This old market town, the birthplace in 1564 of William Shakespeare, has become one of the world's most famous tourist attractions. The splendid half-timbered 16th-century house where the dramatist was born has been a place of literary pilgrimage for nearly 300 years. Also on the Shakespeare trail is New Place or Nash's House, the site of Shakespeare's family home from 1597 until his death. The house was destroyed in 1759, but the picturesque garden has been planted as an Elizabethan knot garden. Hall's Croft, a lovely gabled Tudor house with a walled garden was the home of Dr John Hall, who married the poet's daughter Susanna. All three properties are open all year. The town also preserves some fine half-timbered houses, a 15th-century 14-arch bridge, a beautiful parish church overlooking the River Avon – Shakespeare's burial place – and the renowned Royal Shakespeare Theatre and Collection.

Weston and Welford-on-Avon: These pretty villages of timbered, thatched cottages are typical of Shakespeare country. Weston is a small cluster of houses with a 15th-century church; Welford is significantly larger, with some fine timbered cottages nestling around an original Saxon church.

Aston Cantlow: The church here is reputedly the one in which John Shakespeare and Mary Arden, Shakespeare's parents, were married in 1557. The rest of the village boasts a pleasing mixture of timbered houses, including The Kings Arms and the fine 15th-century Guildhall, part of which was once used as the village gaol.

Wilmcote: The highlight of this village is the magnificent timbered farmhouse that was the home of Mary Arden. Simply furnished, the house, surrounded by a charming, old-fashioned cottage garden, retains a strong sense of atmosphere, enhanced by the collection of old Warwickshire agricultural implements housed in nearby stone barns.

Shottery: A pretty little hamlet across the fields from Stratford, Shottery is famous for the idyllic thatched and timbered cottage where Anne Hathaway lived, and where Shakespeare came to woo her. Its rooms contain original Tudor furniture and fascinating domestic items from life in 16th-century England. The Hathaway family lived in the house from 1470 until 1911. In spring and summer the cottage gardens are ablaze with flowers, including some fine roses. (All open all year.)

WHAT TO LOOK OUT FOR

On entering Welford-on-Avon note the splendid maypole on the village green. It stands 65 feet (20m) tall and is one of only five in the country. A maypole has stood here since the 14th century; the present pole is painted red, white and blue and sports a running fox weather vane on its top.

The unexceptional Victorian parish church in Binton is worth a closer look for the great west window, which illustrates and commemorates the last tragic voyage of Captain Robert Scott to the Antarctic. Scott spent his last few days in England here, bidding farewell to his brother-in-law, the Reverend Lloyd Bruce, who was rector of the parish, before leaving for the South Pole in 1910.

The Tissington Trail from Ashbourne to Hartington

RIDE 25
STAFFORDSHIRE
SK176469

INFORMATION

Total Distance
26 miles (41.5km),
with 22 miles (35.5km) off-road

Grade
1

OS Map
Landranger 1:50,000 sheet 119
(Buxton, Matlock & Dove Dale)

Tourist Information
Ashbourne, tel: 01335 343666; Peak

The Tissington Trail is a straightforward route along a disused railway line, incorporating tarmac and rolled shale surface, suitable mainly for hybrid mountain bikes. There are lovely views of the limestone countryside of the White Peak – and despite that name, the route is fairly level, making this route a leisurely traffic-free ride that can be enjoyed by all the family.

National Park Office, Bakewell,
tel: 01629 816200

Cycle Shop/Hire
Peak Cycle Hire, Ashbourne,
tel: 01335 343156

Nearest Railway Station
Uttoxeter (12 miles/19.5km)

Refreshments
Pubs and cafés in Ashbourne and Hartington; cafés on the Trail at Tissington and Alsop; several picnic spots along the Trail

Spring greenery, Tissington Estate

START & ROUTE DIRECTIONS

Start

Ashbourne, just outside the Peak District National Park, is situated at the crossing of the A515 and A52, between Derby and Stoke-on-Trent. Park in the designated car park for the Tissington Trail, north-west of the town centre on Mappleton Lane.

Directions

1 ⬲ From the car park, join this – the southern – end of the Tissington Trail, and set off northwards towards Tissington. For the first 2 miles (3km) the route is mainly lined with trees, offering great places for woodland birds. After about 3 miles (5km) at Thorpe, there is a pleasant picnic site. You are now inside the southern boundary of the Peak District National Park. Continue along the route and cross over the A515 to reach the village of Tissington.

2 ⬲ Bear left to explore Tissington. Facilities here include toilets and a café. Return to the trail and continue northwards. After about 1 mile (1.5km) the trees open out to reveal the rolling Derbyshire landscape with its appealing drystone walls, its valleys and hills. Pass a hotel on the left, and reach the car park at Alsop.

3 ⬲ From here a footpath lies eastward to the little hamlet of Alsop en le Dale, or you can explore the lane westward which leads to the northern tip of scenic Dove Dale. Return to the Tissington Trail and

The Trail uses a former railway line

continue northwards, passing under the A515 and following the curve of the hill round. Pass over a minor road and continue through a cutting, with the little hill of Johnson's Knoll on the left. Stay on the trail passing the settlements of Greenhead and Biggin on the left. Pass under a minor road and through a cutting to reach the car park just before the B5054.

4 ⬲ The Tissington Trail continues northward to Parsley Hay and beyond, but leave the route here and turn left along the B5054 for the steep descent into Hartington. Take time to explore before retracing your route back up the hill. Rejoining the Tissington Trail turn south.

The market square, Ashbourne

Retrace the outward route
back into the centre of
Ashbourne, enjoying the views
from the opposite direction.
Note: the Tissington Trail is
used not only by cyclists but
also by walkers and horse
riders, and consideration must
be given to other trail users.

Stopping for a break...

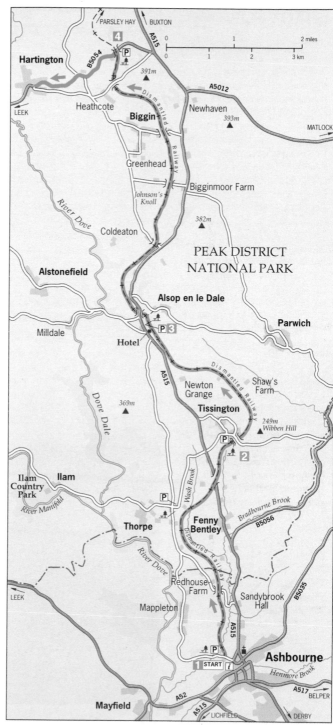

PLACES OF INTEREST

WHAT TO LOOK OUT FOR

Disused railway tracks can be a stable refuge for all sorts of wildlife, and the Tissington Trail is no exception.
Look out particularly for wild flowers, including meadow cranesbill, wild thyme, harebell and even occasional patches of heather – a reminder that this area was once covered by heath. Look out for birds, too, including wheatears and springtime flocks of lapwings.

Ashbourne: The old market town has always been an important commercial centre, at the point where so many routes meet, and its prosperity may be seen among the splendid Georgian buildings of Church Street. Ashbourne was admired by the novelist George Eliot, and Dr Johnson was a regular visitor. In the church, look out for the memorial to young Penelope Boothby, fluent in four languages, who died at the tender age of five.

Ashbourne is perhaps most famous for its very own annual Shrovetide Football game, played over a three-mile 'pitch', when the Up'ards (those inhabiting the ground north of the Henmore Brook) take on the Down'ards (those living to the south).

The Tissington Trail: The former railway line runs for 13 miles (21km) from Ashbourne to Parsley Hay, where it links up with the scenic High Peak Trail. The original railway was constructed towards the end of the railway boom in 1899, and never ran at its hoped-for capacity. However, today its trail provides a popular route for walkers and cyclists through the limestone scenery of the southern Peak District.

Tissington: The attractive village which gave its name to the Tissington Trail is synonymous with the old Derbyshire tradition of well-dressing, when elaborate floral designs are created, usually with a religious theme, to decorate local wells. The ceremony at Tissington is one of the oldest and dates back to the middle of the 14th century; there are five wells here, including a 'children's' well, and dressing takes place around Ascension Day.

Hartington: This pleasing town is built around an unusually wide square, and is set in some of the loveliest scenery in Derbyshire. The limestone landscape is littered with prehistoric burial sites and ancient earthworks, and there are signs too of the lead-mining on which the town once prospered.

By the pond at Tissington

Oakham and Rutland Water

RIDE 26
LEICESTERSHIRE
SK860088

This ride uses lanes to the south of Rutland Water through gently rolling countryside, with some short steep hills. There is some fine scenery, with unique landmarks. On the return the ride skirts the eastern and northern shores of Rutland Water on solid, crushed limestone tracks away from the traffic.

INFORMATION

Total Distance
27 miles (43km)
with 8 miles (13km) off-road

Grade
2

OS Map
Landranger 1:50,000 sheet 141
(Kettering & Corby)

Tourist Information
Rutland Water (summer only),
tel: 01780 460321

Cycle Hire
Rutland Water Cycling, Whitwell,
tel: 01780 460705

Nearest Railway Station
Oakham

Refreshments
Various pubs,
tea rooms and cafés
in Oakham;
on the route there are
The Horse and Jockey pub at Manton,
and The Fox and Hounds at
North Luffenham;
numerous good picnic spots beside
Rutland Water

A fountain stands in the market square at Uppingham

START & ROUTE DIRECTIONS

Start

Oakham lies in the Vale of Catmose on the A606 between Melton Mowbray, 9 miles (14.5km) to the north and Stamford, 10 miles (16km) to the east. Use the South Street car park behind the Rutland County Museum.

Directions

1 🚲 Leave Oakham on the A606 Stamford road and after ¾ mile (1km) turn right. After ¼ mile (0.5km) turn right again, towards Egleton, with the spire of Egleton church ahead. Pass on through the village to a junction at the nature reserve. Turn left onto a cycle track which follows Rutland Water's western shore for 1 mile (1.5km), to meet the A6003 at Sounding Bridge.

2 🚲 Keeping to the cycle track, go under the railway bridge and through a gate to Manton. At the top of the hill go straight across and continue for 1½ miles (2.5km)

to the village of Wing. Bear left towards Morcott, pass The Cuckoo Inn and turn right after the church and before the maze, towards Glaston. Continue on this road, turning right at the next junction. After ½ mile (1km) turn left. Keep straight on over crossroads, to reach a junction with the A47 at the top of a steep hill.

3 🚲 Turn right on to the A47 and immediately left to go into Uppingham. Leave Uppingham along the Seaton road, and continue straight on to reach the village of Seaton in 2½ miles (4km). Pause at the crossroads after The George and Dragon Inn for a panoramic view of the Welland Valley, Harringworth village and the 82-arch railway viaduct. Carry straight on to cross the railway, and after 1 mile (1.5km), turn left towards Morcott. A windmill stands on the hill to the east of the village. At the A47 turn right and then left into Morcott

Normanton Church, Rutland Water

village, and go left again at The White Horse Inn.

4 🚲 At the western end of the village turn right towards North Luffenham. After 1½ miles (2.5km) cross the railway, and continue into North Luffenham. Bear right and follow this road through the village. Pass The Fox and Hounds Inn, and turn left at the next junction towards Edith Weston. Pass the entrance to the RAF base and turn right into the Normanton road, signed 'Rutland Water'. After ½ mile (1km) turn left into the Normanton picnic area beside Rutland Water.

5 🚲 Follow the cycle track anti-clockwise round the reservoir, passing the preserved Normanton church (now a museum) on its protective stone base. After 1 mile (1.5km) turn left across the dam, with Empingham village on the right. Follow the waymarked track along the north shore of the reservoir, passing Sykes Lane picnic area, and the Sailing

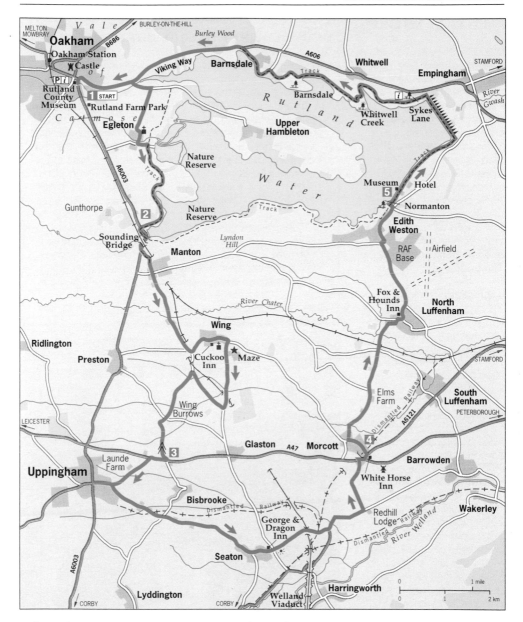

Lodge, and Harbour restaurant at Whitwell Creek. Continue along the short path through woodland for 1 mile (1.5km) to the Barnsdale picnic area, with its nearby arboretum and special

drought garden. Follow the metalled road for ½ mile (1km), and at the junction turn left on to the waterside cycle track. After ½ mile (1km) join the roadside (A606) metalled

cycle/footpath, which is the last section of the 100-mile (160km) Viking Way from the Humber Bridge to Oakham. Follow this for 2 miles (3km) back into Oakham.

PLACES OF INTEREST

Oakham: The pleasant old county town of ancient Rutland has a fine 12th-century Norman hall (the Castle) which is full of ceremonial horseshoes surrendered by royalty and peers of the realm who have passed through the town. Rutland County Museum contains a fascinating collection of artefacts portraying the life and history of Rutland. Within a short distance is Rutland Farm Park, a working farm with rare and commercial breeds of cattle, picnic facilities and a nature trail.

Uppingham: The town stands high among rolling countryside, with superb views around. Its attractive, unspoilt stone and Collyweston-slated buildings surrounding the ancient market place make it a photographer's delight. The original Uppingham School building of 1584 stands beside the church. The town is now noted for its antique and book shops.

Rutland Water: This huge reservoir has become a recreational facility of enormous importance. Its provision includes fishing, water sports, water cruises, and a butterfly and aquatic centre. The cyclist has access to many miles of off-road tracks, and binoculars are essential. The Water is both a Site of Special Scientific Interest and a Ramsar site (of international importance for bird life). There are nature reserves at Egleton and Lyndon Hill.

The old square at the heart of the little town of Oakham

WHAT TO LOOK OUT FOR

Rutland Water is a remarkable place for birds – from grey herons to tiny dabchicks – and there are three easily accessible parts of the cycle route from which to see them: from the Barnsdale (A606) cycle path; over Sounding Bridge (A6003); and at the Egleton Bird Watching Centre with its several hides, the latter requiring a fee. From the cycle track by the reserve notice the many unusual shrubs including dogwood, snowberry, guelder rose, spiraea and barberry. At Whitwell Creek look out for the Great Tower of Alexander (1980) along the shore and the 91st birthday tribute stone to Dame Sylvia Crowe, the landscape architect of Rutland Water.

Lyndon Hill nature reserve is excellent for wild flowers including several species of orchid, bulrush, purple loosestrife, corn cockle, greater mullein and corn marigold. On a sunny day these blooms will be awash with butterflies including large skipper, Essex skipper, gatekeeper, painted lady, ringlet and small tortoiseshell.

Note the medieval turf maze on the road from Wing to Glaston.

Alford and the South Lincolnshire Wolds

This ride combines winding lanes on flat land with the gently rolling countryside of the south Lincolnshire Wolds. Only two or three short hills are taxing on this route, which is predominantly along quiet lanes with magnificent views.

RIDE 27
LINCOLNSHIRE
TF455761

INFORMATION

Total Distance
21½ miles (34.5km)

Grade
2

OS Map
Landranger 1:50,000 sheet 122
(Skegness)

Tourist Information
Alford (summer only),
tel: 01507 462143;
Louth, tel: 01507 609289

Cycle Shop
James Cycles, Alford, tel: 01507
463329

Nearest Railway Station
Skegness (15 miles/24km)

Refreshments
Plenty of pubs and tea rooms
in Alford;
pubs along the route include
The Vine at South Thoresby, and
The Gate at Ulceby;
at Stockwith Mill, near
Hagworthingham,
a tea room serves summer teas
and buffet lunches

*The great windmill at Alford is a
good landmark*

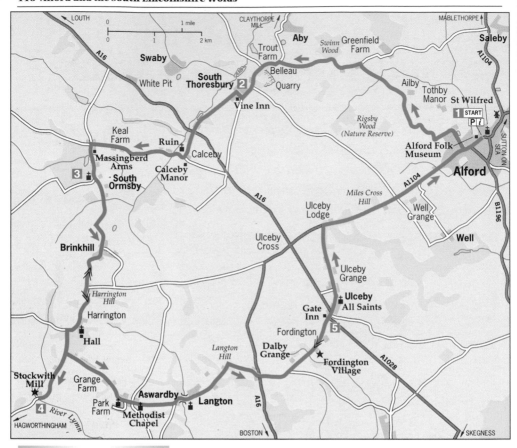

Langton Church

Start

Alford lies on the coastal plain at the southern edge of the Lincolnshire Wolds. It is 15 miles (24km) south-east of Louth by the A16 and the A1104 and 6 miles (10km) from the east coast at Sutton on Sea. Begin the ride from the South Market Place car park, behind the library.

Directions

1 ⬲ Leave the town centre heading south-west along West Street, and turn right into Tothby Lane. Follow this winding, level road for 2 miles (3km) and turn left towards Aby. Continue to a T-junction. Turn left away from Aby, and keep left towards South Thoresby. Pass a turning to Belleau and continue up a short rise, between conifer plantations, with a limestone quarry on the left. Carry on across the next junction and soon turn right, at The Vine Inn, into South Thoresby.

2 ⬲ Follow the road through the village and continue, to meet the A16 at a staggered junction. Go straight across, with care, and

follow the road down to Calceby Manor. Turn right, with the ruins of Calceby church behind and above you as you turn. Climb a long, shallow hill for 1¼ miles (2km) and turn left at The Massingberd Arms, towards South Ormesby. Continue, to enter the village, with the old school and church on the right.

3 ڶ Fork left here, passing the fine thatched Bishop's Cottage on the left, and continue for 1 mile (1.5km) into Brinkhill. Continue through the village and after ½ mile (1km) and a short steep climb, bear right towards Harrington. Pass the Hall (the church is hidden among trees nearby) turn left. At the next junction follow signs towards Hagworthingham, and after another ¾ mile (1km) reach Stockwith Mill.

4 ڶ Retrace your route back to the last junction and turn right towards Aswardby. At the crossroads in Aswardby keep straight on, passing a tiny Methodist chapel on the right. After ½ mile (1km) turn left into Langton with its packhorse bridge beside the red-brick church. Go through the village and climb up through mixed woodland for almost a mile, with superb views back across the Wolds and forward to the North Sea. Cross the A16 with care, and continue through Fordington, to climb a short, steep hill leading up to the A1028.

5 ڶ Bear left at The Gate Inn, and shortly right into Ulceby village, passing the red-brick church of All Saints on the right. (This building dates from 1826, the previous thatched church having burned down.) Go through Ulceby, and in 1 mile (1.5km) reach the A1104. Turn right here for a welcome 2½ mile (4km)

downhill ride to Alford. There are superb views from this road across to the sea some 6 miles (10km) away to the east. Continue straight ahead in Alford to return to the car park and the start point.

Stockwith Mill lies on the River Lymm

Market day in Alford

PLACES OF INTEREST

Alford: This busy market town occupies a favourable position in flat countryside some 6 miles (10km) from the sea and 2 miles (3km) from the Lincolnshire Wolds.
Its narrow streets of Georgian and Victorian houses and shops are arranged around the 14th-century church of St Wilfrid and a spacious double market place. On summer Fridays a craft market with up to 90 stalls is extremely popular.
Among the town's old buildings the thatched manor house, a timber-framed property dating from 1540, houses the Alford Folk Museum.
Waters from the Wolds flow through Alford along the river Woldgrift and its tributary the Mill Rundle. A permissive footpath along the latter is part of two walks, one of 4 miles (6.5km) around the town and one of 7 miles (11km) into open countryside towards the Wolds. The five-sailed commercial working mill, built in 1837, where organic wholemeal flour is ground and sold, must not be missed. Among nearby attractions, the water mill at Claythorpe may be visited by taking a 2 mile (3km) diversion from the described route just before South Thoresby.

South Ormsby Church: The glass in the south aisle window of this church came from Notre Dame in Paris during the French Revolution.

Stockwith Mill: Hoe Hill, Black Hill, Nab Hill and Tetford all feed water into the lovely River Lymm, flowing down the valley eastwards by Hagworthingham. Here lies Stockwith Mill. It would be difficult to find as tranquil a spot as Stockwith, in all England. The tea room and craft shop are open from March to October. Homemade food is served by the mill pool, the water wheel and the mill race. There are three waymarked country walks, of which the longest is 1 mile (1.5km), and it is not unusual to see a kingfisher along the river.

The Folk Museum, Alford

WHAT TO LOOK OUT FOR

There are things of interest in all of the tiny villages along the route, so take time to explore. Find the church at Aswardby (along Post Office Lane) and go beyond the western boundary of the tree-lined graveyard to see an unusual line of animal graves. Look for Harrington church with its tower and 'ting-tang' bell, and a carpet at the altar which was used in Westminster Abbey for the Queen's Coronation in 1953. At Langton notice the noble three-decker pulpit and the unusual inward-facing box pews; both Dr Johnson, the great English scholar, and Sir John Betjeman, loved and admired this church.

RIDE 28
STAFFORDSHIRE
SK103594

The Manifold Way and Ilam

The first 8 miles (13km), from Hulme End to Waterhouses, are along the popular Manifold Way, one of the best 'off-highway' cycling routes in the country. It is surfaced throughout, and only a short section between Swainsley and Wettonmill is shared with light traffic. Riders wanting a really easy day might return along the trail from Waterhouses to Hulme End. Beyond Waterhouses, the main route climbs to open country before descending to Ilam, one of Staffordshire's loveliest villages. The return ride offers a diversion to visit Milldale at the head of Dovedale.

Cyclists on the Manifold Way at Hulme End

INFORMATION

Distance
20 miles (32km),
with 8 miles (13km) off-road

Grade
2

OS Map
Landranger 1:50,000 sheet 119
(Buxton, Matlock & Dove Dale)

Tourist Information
Buxton, tel: 01298 25106

Cycle Shops/Hire
Brown End Farm, Waterhouses,
tel: 01538 308313;
Peak Cycle Hire, Waterhouses,
tel: 01538 308609;
Parsley Hay Cycle Hire
(Tissington Trail),
tel: 01298 84493

Nearest Railway Station
Buxton
(10 miles/16km)

Refreshments
The Manifold Valley Hotel at Hulme
End serves pub meals,
and children are welcome at
The George;
tea rooms at Wettonmill and
Lea Farm;
café at Ilam Hall;
tea rooms in Alstonfield

START & ROUTE DIRECTIONS

Start

Hulme End lies in the south-west corner of the Peak District National Park, on the B5054, 2 miles (3km) west of Hartington between Buxton and Ashbourne. Park in the car park at the start of The Manifold Way (honesty box for payment).

Directions

1 🚲 From the back of the car park, turn on to the Manifold Way cycle route, heading south. In 1 mile (1.5km) at Ecton cross over the byroad (gates) and continue along the Trail with Ecton Hill on the left. At Swainsley the route passes through a well-lit tunnel. From here the trail is also used by light motor traffic, so care is required. Continue along the route to reach Wettonmill.

2 🚲 At Wettonmill there is a choice of ways: either continue on the Trail, or fork right through a ford on the 'old' road. The routes re-join in ½ mile (1km) at Redhurst Crossing - turn through the gate here and continue along the trail following the windings of the River Manifold. Continue to reach a junction at Weag's Bridge. A steep road on the right leads to the pretty village of Grindon. Cross over the lane, pass through a gate and continue along the Manifold Way. This soon leaves the River Manifold and turns instead along the valley of its tributary, the River Hamps. Stay on the trail along the

valley, passing woodland on the steep flank of Soles Hill to the left. Continue, and near a disused quarry, come out at the A523 near Waterhouses.

3 🚲 Turn left with care on to the busy A523 towards Ashbourne. Climb for ½ (1km) and take the first turning left on to a byroad. On the outskirts of Calton village turn left, and turn left again in ½ mile (1km), heading

Beeston Tor, near Weag's Bridge

north. Climb into open country and descend, to reach Throwley Hall in 2 miles (3km). Pass through the gates and yard of Throwley Hall then continue along the lane. Descend and bear left to cross a bridge over the River Manifold. Climb to T-junction with Ilam Country Park on the right. Turn right and descend into Ilam.

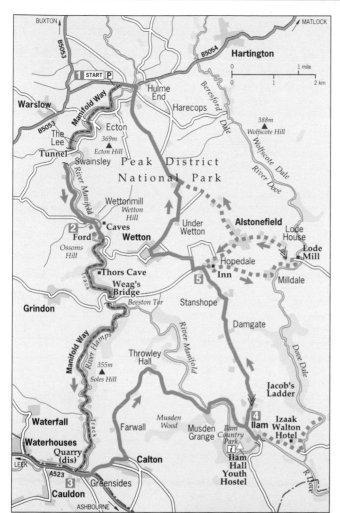

Turn right here, and descend into Hopedale.

5 🚲 For a hilly but scenic diversion to the route here, turn almost immediately right, pass the inn, and continue to Milldale. Bear left in Milldale beside the River Dove, and at Lode Mill turn sharply left and climb steeply into Alstonefield. Turn right at the village green towards Hulme End, and meet up again with the main route which joins this road from Wetton.

To continue on the main route go back through Hopedale and turn right, and then shortly bear left towards Wetton. Keep left and then turn right to explore the village. Leave Wetton, heading north-east towards Hulme End, passing prehistoric burial sites on Wetton Hill to the left. At the junction, turn left, and in 2 miles (3km) reach the B5054 at Hulme End. Turn left, and left again to return to the car park.

The Manifold Valley Hotel at Hulme End is a popular spot for refreshments

4 🚲 From Ilam you can stay on this road and turn left by the Izaak Walton Hotel to explore the foot of scenic Dove Dale.

Otherwise, retrace the route back through Ilam and keep right at the junction towards Hopedale and Alstonefield. Climb steeply for 1 mile (1.5km) then continue into open country. Keep left at Stanshope, and descend to a T-junction.

PLACES OF INTEREST

Hulme End: The car park is the original site of the terminus station and engine sheds of the Manifold Valley Light Railway, which was closed in 1934. It was constructed to carry milk from the surrounding farms but also operated a passenger service. Its route today provides a popular walking and cycling route, The Manifold Way.

Wettonmill: This beautiful spot is well worth a pause, if only to explore the caves in the hillside opposite. There is also a small tea room, toilets, and a camp site. The River Manifold disappears underground here into 'swallets', and except after heavy rainfall, does not reappear until it reaches Ilam.

Weag's Bridge: A picturesque stone bridge crosses the river

WHAT TO LOOK OUT FOR

The pale-coloured, porous limestone rock found in this area of the Peak District has given it the name of the 'White Peak'; if you look carefully at boulders in the drystone walls you may see signs of fossilised plants and animals.

here, below the lofty heights of Beeston Tor. A steep road leads up to the village of Grindon; in the church there is a memorial to an RAF crew who were killed when their plane crashed while dropping food supplies at a time when the village was cut off by snow.

Ilam: Ilam is one of the most beautiful villages in Staffordshire, with an unusually tall gothic cross and a pleasing bridge over the River Manifold, which reappears here after flowing underground from Wettonmill. Ilam is a model

village, largely rebuilt during the 19th century. Its attractive country park is in the care of the National Trust, and the Old Hall is a popular Youth Hostel. This is also the gateway to the beautiful Dove Dale area.

Wetton: This pleasing old village of stone cottages is a good centre for exploring this part of the Peak District. A ½ mile (1km) walk leads to the dramatic Thor's Cave, a vast cavern overlooking the Manifold Valley and once inhabited.

Wettonmill on the River Manifold

The Golden Valley and Black Mountains

RIDE 29
HEREFORD & WORCESTER
SO344385

An adventurous ride along peaceful and generally well-surfaced lanes starts easily, leading along the Golden Valley to Dorstone. One big climb then takes you in just 3 miles (5km) high up to a road over the Black Mountains, before a series of long descents along secluded valleys brings you back to Peterchurch.

INFORMATION

Total Distance
17½ miles (28km)

Grade
3

OS Map
Landranger 1:50,000 sheet 161
(Abergavenny & The Black Mountains)

Tourist Information
Hereford, tel: 01432 268430

Cycle Shops/Hire
Joyrides (hire/repair), Peterchurch,
tel: 01981 550316;
Coombes Cycles (also hire), Hereford,
tel: 01432 354373;
Mastercraft Cycles, Hereford,
tel: 01432 274047;

Nearest Railway Station
Hereford (13 miles/21km)

Refreshments
In Peterchurch there are
The Old Bakery Tearooms, The
Broughton Arms and The Nag's Head;
along the route, try the ancient,
delightful Pandy Inn in Dorstone,
or The Bridge Inn at
Michaelchurch Escley;
there is a good picnic spot at
Vowchurch.

The ride explores the lovely region of the Golden Valley

START & ROUTE DIRECTIONS

Start

The ride starts from the village of Peterchurch, which lies on the B4348 in the Golden Valley, between Hereford and Hay-on-Wye. The public car park and picnic area are opposite the church: turn off the B4348 at The Broughton Arms.

Directions

1 🚲 Turn right out of the car park and, keeping the church on your left, walk through the gate and over the bridge. Turn left alongside the river, then immediately bear round to the right and follow the public footpath beside a small brook until it joins a track. Mount up and follow this track up to the road, bearing right to reach the crossroads. Carry straight on towards Dorstone. Continue for 2 miles (3km) along the lane to Dorstone, passing some old lime kilns in a field on your left after about ½ mile (1km).

2 🚲 In Dorstone, the village green has seats around a drinking fountain, and a sundial on a stone column, with The Pandy Inn just opposite. Keep to the left of the village green, and in ¼ mile (0.5km), just before joining the B4348, turn left into a lane towards Mynydd Brith. Stay on this road and climb for 2 miles (3km); then, where the road goes on to Archenfield, turn left towards Michaelchurch. Beware of steep gradients up and down. Pass through two farmyards, turning to the left each time, and look out for over-enthusiastic sheep dogs. At the T-junction turn right towards Michaelchurch, and a final, very steep ½ mile (1km) climb past woodland brings you to the top. You can take in the view across Wales while you rest.

3 🚲 Turn left at the T-junction towards Michaelchurch. There is a good view ahead of the western edge of the Black Mountains as you continue over the very highest point; at 1,400ft (427m) this is the third highest road over these mountains. Continue for 5 miles (8km) along a generally falling road, with a couple of sudden sharp corners, following the course of the Escley Brook to reach Michaelchurch Escley.

4 🚲 Continue straight on for ½ mile (1km) to The Bridge Inn, just past the church and down a track on the left, for refreshment if needed. Return to the crossroads and turn right towards Vowchurch. Continue straight on at the next crossroads, to begin a 2

The tall spire of St Peter's at Peterchurch is a fibre-glass replacement

Map showing the route through The Golden Valley and Black Mountains, with locations including ARCHENFIELD, HAY-ON-WYE, Arthur's Stone, Gannols, Dorstone, Old Castle Mound, Cwm Farm, Pandy Inn, Mynyddbrydd, Nant-y-Bar, Draen Farm, Snodhill, Mynydd Brith, Snodhill Castle (remains), Lime Kilns, Golden, Tyuchaf, Vagar Hill, Fine Street, Peterchurch, Cefn Hill, Caeiron, Hinton, Llanrosser, Fairfield High School, Poston Court Farm, Escley Brook, Lower House Farm, Cothill Farm, Turnastone, HEREFORD, The Quakers, Vowchurch, New House Farm, Firs Farm, Lower House Farm, White House, Chanstone Wood, The Black Mountains, Grove Farm, Michaelchurch Court, Bank Farm, Upper Maes-coed, Great Wood, MONMOUTH, Michaelchurch Escley, Bridge Inn

mile (3km) downhill stretch. Continue through Turnastone (look out for a green enamel 'Raleigh Cycles' advertising sign as you pass an old garage on the right), and carry on across the route of the disused railway, over the River Dore and through Vowchurch. Turn left on to the main road towards Hay-on-Wye at the T-junction.

⑤ 🚲 Continue for 1½ miles (2.5km) on the B4348. Immediately after the 30mph sign as you enter Peterchurch, turn left into a lane. In a short distance take the first turning right to pass

Fairfield High School. In ½ mile (1km) you will have completed the circuit; turn sharp right down the track you came up earlier, dismount and rejoin the

public footpath, and walk back over the bridge to return to the car park.

Cottages on the village green at Dorstone

Look out for the old sign for Raleigh bicycles on the side of a house in Turnastone

---

WHAT TO LOOK OUT FOR

An old castle mound near Mynydd Brith can be clearly seen from the top of the hill.

PLACES OF INTEREST

Peterchurch: Peterchurch is a convenient start and end point for the ride, lying on the B4348, with several refreshment places, a car park and even a cycle hire business, yet it remains a simple rural village.

The substantial Norman church has a fibre-glass replacement spire perched on top – thus its grey colour. A wooden panel representing a fish with a chain round its neck hangs over the south door.

Dorstone: This picturesque village is unusual for the area in being compactly arranged around a pleasant triangular village green. The 17th-century village inn is said to lie on the site of an earlier inn built in 1185 by Richard le Breton, one

of the assassins of Thomas á Becket. A steep lane from Dorstone leads 1 mile (1.5km) north to Arthur's Stone, a prehistoric tomb dating from 2,000 BC. The view from here is magnificent.

The Black Mountains: So-called because of their dark appearance from the English side, these great mountains form a formidable barrier along part of the Welsh border. There is a strong contrast between the rugged mountain farms and the lush pastures of the Golden Valley, and the former strategic importance of this boundary is shown by the numerous castle mounds in the area.

Michaelchurch Escley: Hidden up in the Black Mountains, perhaps one of the

most delightful surprises here is the little bridge over a trout stream, down the end of the lane as you approach the village inn.

The entire village was, until comparatively recently, owned by the former occupier of nearby Michaelchurch Court.

Vowchurch and Turnastone: The two fascinating but contrasting old village churches of Vowchurch and Turnastone are set unusually close together on opposite sides of the River Dore. The 14th-century church at Vowchurch has a fine Jacobean screen and an unusual roof, supported by oak posts within the building, rather than by the walls.

The course of the old railway which used to run right along the Golden Valley from Hereford to Hay-on-Wye is clearly visible here, and there is also a picnic site.

Tenby and the Pembrokeshire Coastline

The coastline between Saundersfoot and Pembroke is one of the most beautiful in Britain. Although the route rarely keeps close company with the cliffs and beaches, it does often turn towards the coastline. The views from the high ground are extensive, more than justifying the occasional climbs. Along the way are two impressive castles – at Manorbier and Pembroke – and there are many picturesque corners to explore.

RIDE 30
DYFED
SN134005

INFORMATION

Total Distance
25 miles (40km)

Grade
2

OS Map
Landranger 1:50,000 sheet 158
(Tenby)

Tourist Information
Tenby,
tel: 01834 842402

Cycle Hire
D Brown, Tenby,
tel: 01834 842993

Nearest Railway Stations
Tenby and Pembroke

Refreshments
Both Tenby and Pembroke
have an ample supply of cafés,
restaurants and pubs.
Along the route there are several
pubs including
The Dial Inn at Lamphey
(children welcome), and a snack
bar at Freshwater East;
there are also refreshment
facilities at the Manor House
Wildlife & Leisure Park

A massive gateway in the ancient town walls of Tenby

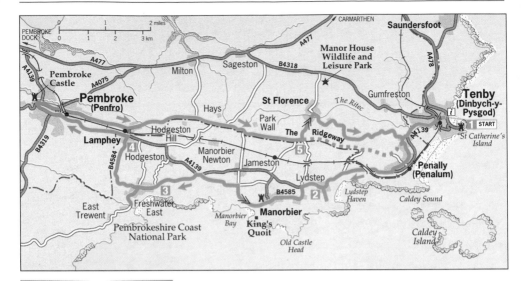

START & ROUTE DIRECTIONS

Start
Tenby is a popular resort located on the South Wales coast 4 miles (6.5km) south of the A477 Carmarthen to Pembroke road, 16 miles (25.5km) south-west of Carmarthen. There is a car park near the railway station.

Looking across to the fortress of St Catherine's Island, Tenby

Directions
[1] 🚲 Leave Tenby by the A4139 towards Pembroke; descend then climb. Turn right on the 'old road' into Penally; continue through the village and after 1 mile (1.5km) rejoin the main road.

Continue for 2½ miles (4km) into Lydstep.

[2] ᛋ For a panoramic viewpoint from Lydstep Haven, turn left and take a by-road down to the entrance of Lydstep Haven Estate. Retrace the route to Lydstep village and turn left. In ½ mile (1km) turn left on to the B4584 signed 'Manorbier'.
In the centre of Manorbier, fork left and descend below the castle walls to the beach. Climb steeply on a narrow by-road and in ½ mile (1km) turn left at the crossroads. In 1 mile (1.5km) at the junction with the A4139, turn left and in 50yds (46m) turn left on a narrow by-road which climbs for 1 mile (1.5km).

[3] ᛋ In a further ½ mile (1km) enter Freshwater East. At the crossroads in the centre of the village you can descend to the lovely beach by turning left. Retrace your route to the crossroads and turn left on to the B4584. In 1½ miles (2.5km) enter Lamphey and, at the junction with the A4139, turn left on to a by-road.

[4] ᛋ Continue, and in 1½ miles (2.5km), shortly after passing Pembroke railway station on the right, turn left and follow the one-way system around the town. In ½ mile (1km) at the Castle entrance, turn right along Main Street. Continue out of town on the A4139. In 2 miles (3km) at Lamphey fork left on a by-road. Climb for

2 miles (3km). From Hodgeston Hill continue along 'The Ridgeway'. In a further 3 miles (5km) turn left at a crossroads for St Florence. (For an alternative and more direct route back to Tenby, continue ahead and descend to Penally and then retrace the outward route). Descend steeply into St Florence.

[5] ᛋ In the centre of the village, at the crossroads by the church turn right and follow a meandering narrow lane through the Ritec Valley for 3 miles (5km) to reach the old road to Penally used on the outward journey. Retrace the route back into Tenby.

The rugged coastline at Manorbier

PLACES OF INTEREST

Tenby: Tenby, in a beautiful location on the west side of Carmarthen Bay, is one of the most delightful coastal resorts in the United Kingdom. There are three sandy beaches, two of them divided by the headland on which stands the remains of a 13th-century castle. On the north side of the headland, there is a picturesque and sheltered harbour which was a busy port in the 17th and 18th centuries. Near by is St Julian's Chapel, also known as the 'Fisherman's Chapel'.

The narrow, quaint streets of the old town are enclosed by 14th-century walls. In Tudor Square stands the 15th-century Tudor Merchant's House which is in the care of the National Trust and is open to the public during the summer months. St Mary's, the largest parish church

in Wales, has a tall spire. Off-shore lies St Catherine's Island, and further out in the bay is Caldey Island on which there is a monastery. Boat trips sail to Caldey Island from the harbour.

Manorbier: Manorbier is built around the moated Norman castle. Although privately owned, the castle and other interesting features, are open to the public during the summer months. It was the birthplace of Giraldus

Cambrensis, the great 12th-century Welsh scholar and topographer.

The route descends below the castle walls to a sandy beach which is ideal for bathing. From the car park, a footpath across the hillside leads to King's Quoit, the standing stones of a pre-historic burial chamber, with a 15ft (4.5m) capstone.

Pembroke: The castle, built in 1207, stands upon a rocky spur above the Pembroke River, which is a creek off Milford Haven, and Henry VII was born here in 1457. The castle has seven towers and a keep 75ft (22.5m) high.

St Florence: This small village nestles in a valley through which the Ritec, a brook, flows to eventually enter the sea near Tenby. The village, once a port, has some old houses with Flemish chimneys. The church contains several interesting monuments. One mile (1.5km) north is Manor House Wildlife and Leisure Park which is set in 35 acres (14ha) wooded grounds and award-winning gardens. Attractions include exotic birds, reptiles and fish, a giant astraglide slide and falconry displays.

Tenby harbour, with its sandy beach

The Black-and-White Villages

This route is an easy, level tour around several of the best best known and most attractive black-and-white villages of Herefordshire. The route threads through a network of quiet, well-surfaced country lanes around Pembridge and Weobley.

INFORMATION

Distance
27 miles (43km)

Grade
1

OS Map
Landranger 1:50,000 sheets 148 (Presteigne & Hay-on-Wye) or 149 (Hereford & Leominster)

Tourist Information
Leominster (summer only),
tel: 01568 616460

Cycle Shops/Hire
Cycle Shop (also hire), Leominster,
tel: 01568 611128;
Coombes Cycles (also hire), Hereford,
tel: 01432 354373;
Mastercraft Cycles, Hereford,
tel: 01432 274047;
Wheely Wonderful Cycling
(hire only), Wigmore,
tel: 01568 770755

Nearest Railway Station
Leominster (7 miles/11.5km)

Refreshments
Eardisland Tea Room, Pembridge Visitor Centre and Jules in Weobley particularly welcome cyclists. Along the route, try The Three Horseshoes at Norton Canon or The Bells Inn, Almeley; and Dunkerton's Cider Mill, Bar and Restaurant, near Pembridge, also serves teas

Standing in spring tulips, the village pump at Almeley

START & ROUTE DIRECTIONS

Start

Pembridge is 7 miles (11km) west of Leominster on the A44 road from Leominster to Kington. Park with care in the village (at the time of writing a public car park is to be built behind the Visitor Centre); the route starts opposite 'Ye Olde Stepppes' shop in the centre.

Directions

[1] 毶 From Pembridge take the road north towards Shobdon and cross the river Arrow. In ½ mile (1km) turn off right into a narrow lane. (This is just before the old railway station on the left, now a private house but still with a railway signal in the garden.) Pass Shobdon airfield on the left. In 2½ miles (4km) at Eardisland turn right to ride through the village. Just after the village turn left into a narrow lane signposted 'Burton Court'.

[2] 毶 Continue, to pass the 18th-century mansion of Burton Court on the right and

cross over the A44 into another narrow lane towards Lower Burton. Continue for ½ mile (1km) passing a small track to the left and bearing right. Turn off left opposite a yellow hydrant and driveway and follow this very narrow lane beside a brook, over a small bridge and up to the main road (A4112). Cross this road with care and go down the small lane opposite, beside a wooden barn. In ¼ mile (0.5km), opposite a pair of garages, turn off left. At the next T-junction turn right and continue for 1 mile (1.5km) into Dilwyn.

[3] 毶 In Dilwyn bear left on to the main road at the

The village green at Dilwyn

The cycle route runs past the lively village mural in Dilwyn

church. Turn left towards Stretford at the village green, then in a short distance turn off right towards Weobley Marsh. After 1½ miles (2.5km) turn right at the T-junction at the top of the rise. In ½ mile (1km) turn left to pass through Weobley Marsh, a traditional village common complete with grazing animals. Just after the common turn off right towards Weobley and in 1 mile (1.5km) go right at the T-junction to enter the village. In Weobley, turn left to enter the village square.

[4] 毶 Ride down the main square, go left and at the T-junction turn left on to the B4230 towards Hereford. (Public toilets are just to the left along this road.) Leave Weobley and in 3 miles (5km) at the A480 turn right towards Lyonshall. In ¼ mile (0.5km) turn left into a lane to Norton Canon. Follow this lane 3½ miles (5.5km) to the main road (A4112) near Kinnersley. Go left at the T-junction here towards Brecon, then shortly turn off right, with care, into the narrow lane to Almeley.

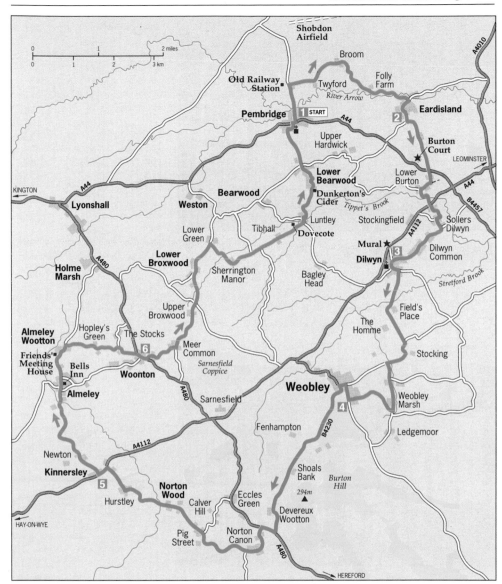

Broom

Twyford

Folly
Farm

River Arrow

Old Railway
Station

Pembridge

1 START

A44

2

Eardisland

Upper
Hardwick

Burton
Court

LEOMINSTER

Lower
Bearwood

Lower
Burton

A4010

Bearwood

Weston

Dunkerton's
Cider

Tippet's Brook

Stockingfield

KINGTON

A44

Lyonshall

Lower
Green

Tibhall

Luntley

Dovecote

Sollers
Dilwyn

A4457

Mural ★

3

Dilwyn
Common

Holme
Marsh

A480

Lower
Broxwood

Sherrington
Manor

Bagley
Head

Dilwyn

A4112

Stretford Brook

Upper
Broxwood

Field's
Place

Almeley
Wootton

Hopley's
Green

The Stocks

6

Meer
Common

*Sarnesfield
Coppice*

The
Homme

Stocking

Friends'
Meeting
House

Bells
Inn

Woonton

A480

Sarnesfield

Weobley

Weobley
Marsh

Almeley

Fenhampton

4

B4230

Ledgemoor

Newton

A4112

Shoals
Bank

*Burton
Hill*

Kinnersley

5

Norton
Wood

Calver
Hill

Eccles
Green

294m ▲

Devereux
Wootton

HAY-ON-WYE

Hurstley

Pig
Street

Norton
Canon

A480

HEREFORD

5 In Almeley carry on past The Bells Inn and straight on past a road to your right. In ¾ mile (1km) beyond the village turn right, beside a stone wall immediately before a green, and follow this narrow lane to join the A480 at Woonton.

6 Go right on to this main road and in a short distance fork left into a lane to Meer and Broxwood. Go left at the next T-junction and continue through Broxwood. In ½ mile (1km) turn off right towards Sherrington, and continue for 2 miles (3km) to Luntley. Go

left here to pass a much-restored dovecote (originally built in 1673), then cross the bridge and turn right towards Dunkerton's Cider. Continue for 2 miles (3km), past the cider company, to return to Pembridge and the start point.

Black-and-white cottages at Dilwyn

PLACES OF INTEREST

Pembridge: It is worth exploring the full length of the village by cycle or on foot. The old wool market, raised on eight oak columns, behind The New Inn is easy to find, but even more interesting is the church, hidden up a nearby flight of steps. Its unusual detached timber bell tower contains a clock whose mechanism can be seen

Fine old timbering in Weobley

WHAT TO LOOK OUT FOR

Dilwyn is a village with the traditional pub and shop facing the village green – but unusually the scene is repeated as a mural in the subway under the north end of the by-pass. To find this, turn right when you get to the church and in ¼ mile (0.5km) walk down the footpath on the left just before the main road.

---

working. A mile to the south is Dunkerton's Cider, a small company making specialist ciders from rare species of apples.

Eardisland: A delightful bridge spans a river populated with hungry ducks and surrounded by immaculate lawns. Look out for the magnificent 14th-century yeoman's hall, Staick House, beside the river. In contrast to the old buildings near the river, the smart timber framed houses and 'dovecote' in a crescent on the right further on through the village are only a few years old. To the south of the village lies Burton Court, an old house largely remodelled in the 19th century, and with a fine collection of historical costumes.

Weobley: Weobley is perhaps the most famous of all the black-and-white villages – even the modern pumping station near the telephone exchange has been disguised as a small black-and-white building. Weobley was once a major town which sent two members to parliament. The large castle mound, reached from the top of the market square, makes a good picnic site for active children.

Almeley: This quiet village offers a seat next to the village pump, and views across to the Black Mountains. Spot the old circular black-and-yellow AA road sign, which tells you that you are exactly 147 miles from London. A mile north is a Friends' (Quaker) Meeting House, purpose built in 1672.

On Wenlock Edge

RIDE 32
SHROPSHIRE
SO450943

INFORMATION

Total Distance
23 miles (37km)

Grade
3

OS Map
Landranger 1:50,000 sheet 137
(Ludlow & Wenlock Edge)

Tourist Information
Ludlow, tel: 01584 875053

Cycle Shops/Hire
Terrys Cycles, Church Stretton,
tel: 01694 724334;
Long Mynd Cycles, Church Stretton,
tel: 01694 722367

Nearest Railway Station
Church Stretton

Refreshments
Cafés at Acton Scott Working Farm,
Carding Mill
and in Church Stretton.
Families welcome at pubs in
Little Stretton and All Stretton,
and at The Crown at Munslow
(open all day summer),
and The Royal Oak at Cardington.
Picnic area in
Wolverton Wood

This attractive ride along winding country lanes in the shadow of the great ridge known as the Long Mynd, starts at Church Stretton, in the beautiful Carding Mill Valley. There is no off-road cycling, but the hills of lowland Shropshire can be demanding.

Enjoying a break at Acton Scott Working Farm

START & ROUTE DIRECTIONS

Start

Church Stretton is a small market town situated on the A49 between Shrewsbury and Ludlow, 12 miles (19km) south of Shrewsbury. Park at the Carding Mill Valley car park, which is signed from the High Street in the town centre.

Directions

1 ⚲ Leave the car park and return to the High Street; turn right on to the B4370 heading south towards Little Stretton. After 1½ miles (2.5km) reach a crossroads with a telephone kiosk on the right. Turn right into Little Stretton, shortly bear left, and then take the right-hand fork towards Minton.

2 ⚲ Reaching Minton, continue up the hill and take the first turning left, bringing you to a T-junction. Turn left here for Marshbrook. At the next t-junction (telephone kiosk on left) turn on to the B4370, which leads straight on to a junction with the A49. Turn right, and after a short distance take the turning on the left to Acton Scott. Continue for ½ mile (1km) and turn right at the crossroads to reach Acton Scott Working Farm.

3 ⚲ Leaving the farm turn left, and after about a mile cross the old railway line and pass through Henley. Continue to Alcaston and follow the road round to the

The beautiful Carding Mill Valley

left. Stay on this road to pass through Wolverton. About 1 mile (1.5km) beyond Wolverton at a T-junction turn right and almost immediately turn left – which feels like doubling back.

Carry on into the hamlet of Middlehope and turn right at the t-junction.

4 ⚲ Continue for nearly 2 miles (3km) to Bache Mill and at the T-junction turn left on to the B4368 towards Much Wenlock. Pass the village of Aston Munslow with the White House Museum on the left, and Munslow, to reach Beambridge. Turn left here, with Millichope Park on the left, signposted to Rushbury. Continue for about ½ mile

on

(1km) to the T-junction and turn left. Stay on this road towards Rushbury for about 1¾ miles (3km), bearing sharp left up Roman Bank to cross the old railway line again and reach the village. Bear right at the fork and go past the old castle mound and Manor Farm. At the B4371 turn left towards Church Stretton, and in a short way turn off right to Cardington.

5 ⮌ Stay on this road for 1½ miles (2.5km) and at the crossroads turn left to enter Cardington. Go straight through the village and follow the signs for Comley. Continue on this road, passing The Lawley hill on the right, to reach a T-junction at Hollyhurst.

Turn left here on to the old Roman road. After about 1 mile (1.5km) at the junction, cross over the A49 and then over the railway, and at the next T-junction turn left on to the B4370 to continue into Church Stretton. After 1½ (2.5km) turn right into the lane leading to Carding Mill Valley, and return to the start of the route.

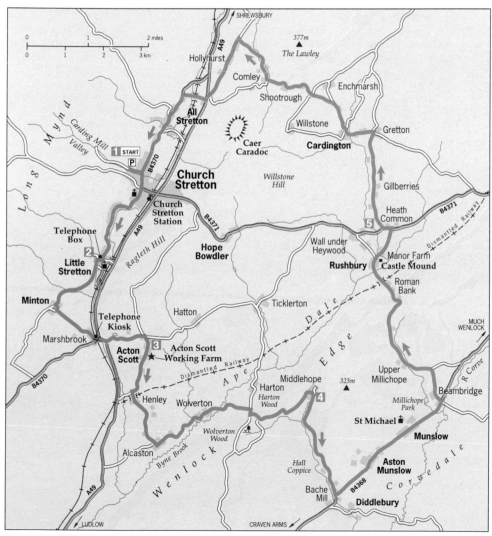

PLACES OF INTEREST

Church Stretton: During the late 19th century the district around this small market town became known as 'Little Switzerland' and the town itself developed into a popular inland resort. Red-brick and half-timbered Victorian villas mingle with older black-and-white buildings to give the town a delightful character complemented by the church, which dates from the 12th century. The lovely Carding Mill Valley stretches up from the village towards the ridge known as the Long Mynd, and the area is warmly recorded in the novels of Mary Webb. Unusually the black-and-white church at nearby Little Stretton is thatched.

The Long Mynd: A fine heather-covered ridge of grits and shales, largely owned and protected by the National Trust, the Long Mynd rises out of the Shropshire lowlands and stretches for about 10 miles (16km). Prehistoric remains on the hill include burial mounds, hill-forts and the ancient Port Way track which traverses its length.

Minton: This little village nestles on the slopes of the Long Mynd. Its name is Saxon in origin, and the remains of a motte can be seen behind the manor house. The village is a charming collection of farms and cottages around a triangular green, and lies on the old trackway that traversed the Long Mynd in the days of the packhorse.

Market day in Church Stretton

WHAT TO LOOK OUT FOR

The B4368 Shipton to Morville road through Corvedale was built by a turnpike trust in the early 19th century. Look out for the mileposts along this straight road, which give the distances to London. Note the former toll-keeper's cottage with gothic windows at Beambridge.

The Church of St Michael at Munslow is worth a detour. The building dates back to 1115, and a most unusual feature is the doorstep of the church, which is a large brick taken from the Great Wall of China.

Acton Scott Historic Working Farm: For a fascinating insight into life on a traditional working farm, visit this working museum. The animals are rare, old-fashioned breeds and the crops are types grown around 1900. All the work on the farm is undertaken by hand, horse-power or with old machines such as steam-threshers (open April to October, not Mondays except Bank Holidays).

Aston Munslow: Legend has it that Dick Turpin, the infamous highwayman, once stayed in the village.

Hidden up a lane north-west of the village is the White House, a 12th-century house of cruck construction with later additions which was home, until 1946, to the Stedman family of bell-ringing fame. The house is now owned by the Landmark Trust.

Caer Caradoc Hill: The earthworks of an Iron-age hill-fort, said to be where British chieftain Caractacus made his last, unsuccessful stand against the Romans in AD50, crown this miniature mountain, which is only 1506ft (459m) high.

RIDE 33
GWYNEDD
SH930362

Bala and the Dee Valley

A lovely ride through one of the most scenically beautiful areas of Britain, this route takes in some strenuous hills as well as flatter valley roads. Although using predominantly minor roads you will encounter very little traffic, for this area is one of the quietest in the country.

INFORMATION

Total Distance
19 miles (31km)

Grade
3

OS Map
Landranger 1:50,000 sheet 125
(Bala & Lake Vyrnwy)

Tourist Information
Bala (summer only),
tel: 01678 520367

Cycle Shop/Hire
R H Roberts, Bala, tel: 01678 520252;
The Cavern, Bala (summer hire),
tel: 01678 521292

*Llyn Tegid (Bala Lake) is the largest
natural stretch of water in Wales*

Nearest Railway Station
Blaenau Ffestiniog (20 miles/32km)

Refreshments
Pubs and tea rooms at Bala;,
also The Bryn Tirion Inn at Llandderfel,
Tyddyn Llan Restaurant,
and The Dudley Arms at
Llandrillo.
Toilets at Bala, Llandrillo
and Llandderfel

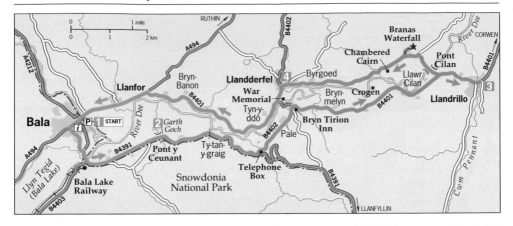

START & ROUTE DIRECTIONS

Start
Bala is situated on the A494 between Dolgellau and Ruthin, on the eastern rim of the Snowdonia National Park. Begin the ride from the car park under the town bridge.

Directions
[1] ۶۶ Turn right out of the car park, then left into Bala High Street. At the traffic lights, turn left into Tegid Street and follow this road across the top of the lake to T-junction. Turn right on to the B4391, cross the River Dee and follow signs for Llangynog. After 3 miles (5km) reach Pont y Ceunant. Immediately after the bridge, on the left is the beauty spot of Garth Goch.

[2] ۶۶ Continue along the B4391 for 2 miles (3km) and turn left at the telephone box, signposted to Corwen (B4402). Descend on this road to reach a T-junction by The Bryn Tirion Inn. Turn

The village of Llandrillo

right, signed 'Corwen', and follow the Dee Valley eastwards. Pass the Crogen Estate and continue straight on to the village of Llandrillo. Follow the road through the village, and as you cross the river bridge, turn immediately left to find an ideal picnic site (also toilets) near the old bridge.

3 ⮂ Retrace your route back through Llandrillo on the B4401. After 1 mile (1.5km)

Garth Goch is a local beauty spot

turn right, signposted 'Branas Isaf', and cross River Dee at Pont Cilan. Continue to a T-junction and turn left onto an unclassified road (can be muddy and wet). After a short distance, the Branas Waterfall can be seen to the right, by a house. (To visit the top of the fall, turn right up the lane, and right again onto the footpath. There is no access to the falls. Return to the main road.)

Stay on this road, passing a chambered cairn on the left, to reach Llandderfel village.

4 ⮂ Turn left at a T-junction, and pass a park on the left. Proceed to the war memorial and turn right, signposted 'Bala'. Follow the route along the River Dee for 3 miles (5km) to meet the A494. Turn left onto the A494, and after 1 mile (1.5km) reach Bala. The car park is on the left as you cross the bridge into the town.

PLACES OF INTEREST

Bala: An old market town with many interesting pubs and buildings, it is also a stronghold of the Welsh language and can seem very 'foreign' to the outsider.

Its lake, Llyn Tegid, is the largest stretch of natural water in the principality, over 4 miles (6.5km) long, and offers canoe hire, sailing and bathing.

The scenic Bala Lake Railway operates along the south side of the lake in summer using steam engines from former Welsh slate quarries.

Garth Goch: This beauty spot, 3 miles (5km) from Bala, was the site of the first sheepdog trials, held here on 9 October 1873. There are splendid views of the surrounding area from the top of the hill.

WHAT TO LOOK OUT FOR

The site of a chambered cairn near the turning to Branas waterfall marks an ancient religion. More recently the area around Bala was famous as a centre of Methodism, and the legacy of chapel buildings can clearly be seen.

The villages of Llandderfel, Llanfor and Llandrillo share the same prefix 'llan', which in Welsh means a holy settlement.

Crogen Estate: Reached 2 miles (3km) before Llandrillo, this is the site of an ancient battle, where Henry II was defeated in 1165 by the Welsh prince Owain Gwynedd. Crogen takes its name from the Celtic word for ferocity, reflecting the nature of the battle.

The estate is private, but there are clear views of the manor house and its surroundings. The Gate House, which you pass on the route, dates from around AD1400.

Llandderfel: The village, on the opposite side of the River Dee, was named after Derfel Gadarn, a 6th-century warrior. There are some interesting carved artefacts in the church. The view across the valley is dominated by Pale Hall (now a hotel and restaurant), which was built in 1870 for Henry Robertson, a successful and wealthy Scottish building engineer.

On the scenic Bala Lake Railway

RIDE 34
CHESHIRE
SJ783696

Goostrey and Alderley Edge

*A gentle ride through prosperous pasturelands.
The lanes are flat to the west, rolling to the east.
The one big climb on to Alderley Edge is avoidable.
Throughout there are delightful contrasts in
landscape and architecture between park and
farm, halls and cottages, old water mills and the
Jodrell Bank radio telescope.*

INFORMATION

Total Distance
27½ miles (44km),.
with ¼ mile (0.5km)
off-road

Grade
2

OS Map
Landranger 1:50,000 sheet 118
(Stoke-on-Trent & Macclesfield)

Tourist Information
Holmes Chapel,
tel: 01477 532441

Nearest Railway Station
Goostrey

Refreshments
Pubs along the route include
The Red Lion at Goostrey
(particularly popular with cyclists)
and The Stag Inn at
Little Warford.
If stopping at the
Jodrell Bank Science Centre
there are refreshment facilities
available.
Alderley Edge is the best
place for a picnic,
fully deserved after the climb
to the top,
and The Wizard Tea Rooms
provide excellent
snacks.

*The woodland at Alderley Edge is in
the care of the National Trust*

START & ROUTE DIRECTIONS

Start

Goostrey is east of Chester, 2 miles (3km) north of Holmes Chapel. It lies between the A50 and A535 and is 4 miles (6.5km) from junction 18 of the M6. Begin the ride from Goostrey Station car park, between Goostrey and Twemlow Green.

Alderley Edge National Trust car park provides an alternative starting point from the north.

Directions:

1 🚴 Turn left out of Goostrey station to Twemlow Green. Go left at the T-junction and then immediately left and right (care needed) over the A535 on to Forty Acre Lane. After 2 miles (3km) turn right, signed 'Swettenham', and in ¾ mile (1km) turn left signed 'Swettenham Heath'. Soon turn left again at a T-junction.

2 🚴 Go over the crossroads towards Marton, on a single track road which becomes Messuage Lane. Turning left at the T-junction join Marton Hall Lane and take the immediate left fork, unsigned, to Marton. Cross the busy A34 with care at Marton, and continue past Pikelow Farm and Trout Pool to the A536 (3 miles/5km). Cross on to Maggoty Lane. Maggoty's Grave is on the left. At the crossroads turn right, and proceed for ¼ mile (0.5km) to

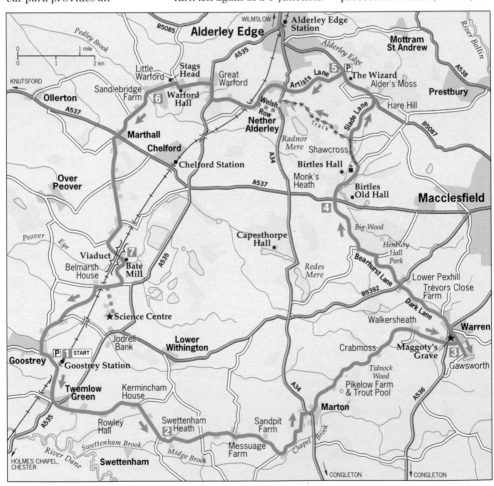

Gawsworth to view the hall and church.

3 🚲 Return to the crossroads and continue into Warren. Cross the A536 with care, following Dark Lane to Lower Pexhill and go right and left over the B5392 on to Bearhurst Lane. At the T-junction turn left and then soon right opposite cottages, signed 'Chelford', skirting Henbury Hall Park.

4 🚲 Cross the A537 on to Birtles Lane and pass Birtles Hall. Immediately after Birtles church, take the tarmac bridleway left. At the three ways in front of farm buildings, take the stony track straight ahead through a gate. The track dips and can be wet in winter but it is only a few yards to a tarmac surface at Shawcross crossroads, where there is a choice.
(To take a short cut, and avoid a climb, go left here on the good cobble and stone byway to Nether Alderley. Here turn left on the A34 and then soon right onto Sand Lane to regain the route at Welsh Row.)
Otherwise, take the road opposite, Slade Lane, and climb on to Alderley Edge. At the T-junction go left on the B5087 for ¾ mile (1km).

5 🚲 Turn left, opposite The Wizard, on Artists Lane, and descend to cross the busy A34 onto Welsh Row at Nether Alderley. Over the bridge, the road becomes Soss Moss Lane. Go right on to the A535 for ¼ mile (0.5km) at Great Warford, then turn left on to

Gawsworth Hall

Merryman's Lane, past Warford Hall, and then almost immediately left again on to Mill Lane past the Stags Head pub. Go through Little Warford and the name of the lane changes to Sandlebridge.

6 🚲 Proceed to Marthall and cross over the A537 with care onto Sandhole/Snelson Lane. Go over the crossroads on to Mill Lane/Boundary Lane, then in 1½ miles (2km) turn left signed 'Bate Mill'. Descend under the little

viaduct to Bate Mill.

7 🚲 Climb to the T-junction and turn right. Jodrell Bank Science Centre is soon on your left. Go left at the T-junction in Goostrey and The Red Lion pub is on the left. Continue on Station Road to return to Goostrey Station car park.

The view across the Cheshire Plain from Alderley Edge is breathtaking

PLACES OF INTEREST

Maggoty's Grave: At the top of Maggoty's Wood is the grave of Samuel (Maggoty) Johnson (1691–1773), who was a dancing master at Gawsworth Hall and the last professional jester in England. His grave carries a long epitaph, thought to be written by himself.

Gawsworth: The village has several fine buidings of note, including a superbly timbered old Rectory.
Gawsworth Hall is a magnificent black-and-white Tudor manor house, viewed to advantage from the road, across the pond (open April to October).
The battlemented church houses the Fitton monuments, with tombs and effigies of four generations of the Fitton family, dating from 1550 to 1643.

Alderley Edge and Artists Lane: Mature beech and oak woods in the care of the National Trust cover this attractive hillside. The most popular view – over the Cheshire and Lancashire plain – is just a short walk from the car park.

Bate Mill: Thi is a complete, original water mill, today in need of restoration. The undershot water wheel was fed from the Peover Eye, ducted under the road, and can be seen through a small window.

The huge radio telescopes at Jodrell Bank dominate the evening skyline

Jodrell Bank Science Centre and Arboretum: Adjacent to the huge Lovell radio telescope, this popular science centre features a famous planetarium and hands-on exhibits.

The arboretum has a wide range of trees and is attractive at any time of the year, and the Environmental Discovery Centre is also well worth exploring (open from March to October, and winter weekends).

WHAT TO LOOK OUT FOR

Traditional black-and-white cottages can be seen along the route, and particularly at Twemlow Green and on Artists Lane. The views are magnificent – check for distant views of the Peak District edges, especially approaching Warren; and there are fine views of Jodrell Bank radio telescope, particularly from the climb to Alderley Edge, the bridge on Welsh Row, and the junction after Bates Mill.
Passing through Warren, note the stone cross stump and pump on the village green.
At Henbury Hall the parkland has renowned bluebell woods in season, while Birtles Hall features a gateway, with mill stones and gears set in the walls.

RIDE 35
WEST/NORTH YORKSHIRE
SE396483

Between
Wharfe and Nidd

This scenic circuit offers much of interest, and options for off-road cycling along the former Wetherby–Spofforth railway. Attractions include two castles to visit, opportunities for boating and looking at rock formations, an ancient wood and panoramic views of Wharfedale.

INFORMATION

Total Distance
28 miles (45km),
with 7 miles (11.5km) off-road

Grade
2

OS Map
Landranger 1:50,000 sheet 104
(Leeds, Bradford & Harrogate)

*The pastoral valley landscape near
Kirkby Overblow*

Tourist Information
Wetherby, tel: 01937 582706;
Knaresborough (summer only),
tel: 01423 866886

Cycle Shop/Hire
Wheels in Motion, High Street,
Wetherby, tel: 01937 588228;
Spa Cycles (hire), Wedderburn Road,
Woodlands, Harrogate,
tel: 01423 887003

Nearest Railway Station
Cattal (7½ miles/12km);
Knaresborough (on route)

Refreshments
Wide selection of cafés,
restaurants and pubs in
Wetherby and Knaresborough;
pubs on the route include
The Railway at Spofforth,
The Radcliffe Arms at Follifoot, and
The Shoulder of Mutton and
The Star and Garter at
Kirkby Overblow;
also The Scott's Arms at Sicklinghall
and The Windmill at Linton,
and The Clapgate Inn
at Kearby
has a children's play area

START &
ROUTE DIRECTIONS

Start

Wetherby lies beside the A1 (currently being upgraded to motorway) 12 miles (19km) north of Leeds and 13 miles (21km) west of York. The ride begins from the old station car park on Linton Road, west of Wharfe Grange; look for the blue cycle route sign.

Directions

1 🚲 Pass through the first barrier on to a cycle path under the steel bridge; fork left where path divides. Continue on this dedicated route for about 3 miles (5km) to Spofforth; turn right onto the A661 along the High Street. Beyond the bend at Castle Inn, turn left by the church, then right up Church Hill to pass The King William IV pub. Take the second turning left into Beech Lane, and go on to the castle (no admission charge).

Knaresborough, from the River Nidd

2 🚲 Continue north on Castle Street and keep right at the fork beyond the village, climbing gradually to Follifoot. Turn right at the T-junction near The Radcliffe Arms, descending to cross Crimple Beck, then rising to the junction with the A661. Turn sharply right here, descend, and turn left to Plompton Rocks (open from March to October). Beyond East Lodge the path is currently a public footpath, therefore *wheel* cycles on the driveway to the north-west corner of Plompton Hall Farm (beware farm vehicles). Now ride on

the bridleway west through a gap in the wall going north, then east and north again along the edge of Birkham Wood to reach a gate at the junction with the A658. Cross with care, pass through the gate opposite, and follow the bridleway round to the right through the wood, and continue on a track at the edge of the lido to reach a wicket gate. Go through onto the A658 and turn left, then take the first exit from the roundabout, into Knaresborough on the B6164. (*Note:* if conditions

are very wet, use the A658 from the first gate to the roundabout.)

3 🚲 At Grimbald Bridge cross the River Nidd and turn immediately left onto Abbey Road (beware of the hump after the first descent). Continue to a junction with the B6163. Go over the crossroads into Waterside; to visit the castle and town centre, walk up the path or by Water Bag Bank, beyond the railway viaduct. Retrace the route on Waterside to the low bridge and turn right onto the B6163, up Bland's Hill. Then

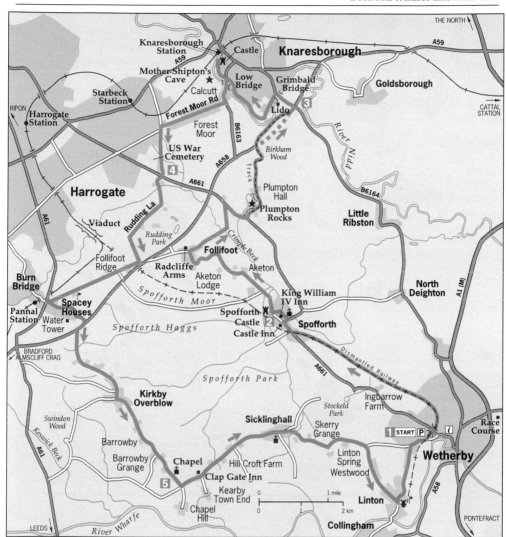

take the second turning right (at a pub) onto Forest Moor Road. In 1 mile (1.5km) turn left at the crossroads to pass the American cemetery, then cross the A661 into Rudding Lane.

4 🚲 Take the descent with care, then climb gradually, passing Rudding Park on the left. At the next junction turn right, signed 'Pannal', and

continue west across Follifoot Ridge to Spacey Houses. At the golf club turn sharp left into Drury Lane and continue to the junction with the A658. Turn right here and immediately left, eventually descending to Kirkby Overblow. In the village turn left at the T-junction, and continue along a ridge, to pass a chapel in about a mile.

5 🚲 Bear left, and keep left at The Clap Gate Inn, continuing north-east to Sicklinghall. Descend through the village, heading towards Wetherby. Beyond Linton Spring, fork right to Linton. In the village turn sharply left opposite The Windmill pub. Pass the golf course, and then turn right at a junction with Linton Lane, returning to the car park in Wetherby.

PLACES OF INTEREST

Wetherby: This old coaching town is situated on the former Great North Road, with a market and racecourse. The town is wholly north of the winding Wharfe, and the riverside is a pleasant recreation area. See the Shambles of 1811 and the Town Hall, built in1845.

Spofforth: Its church is most prominent but is largely noted for having the grave of Blind Jack of Knaresborough, a great 18th-century road and bridge builder. The castle is reputedly the birthplace of Harry Hotspur and comprises well-kept 13-15th-century remains in a sylvan setting.

Plompton Rocks: Amazing rock formations are to be found in a woodland setting around a small deep lake, with a network of attractive paths.

Knaresborough: Located where the Nidd is channelled through a rocky gorge, its town centre with market, castle and ancient chemist's shop is some 120ft (36m) above the river. The castle is an imposing fortress that was once the hiding place for Thomas á Becket's murderers and it also served as a prison for Richard II. Knaresborough is famous for its Dropping Well where water drips on to an overhang, forming a lime deposit which is slowly petrifying a curious assortment of hats, toys, parasols and other objects strung above the rock face by the owners of the cave since the 19th century. Equally popular with visitors is Mother

---

Shipton's Cave where the legendary prophetess was born in July 1488 (she predicted the development of the aircraft).

Sicklinghall: This ancient linear village has an attractive Roman Catholic church, with 12th-centuryTemplar origins .

Linton: Now very much an executive dormitory for Leeds, the village centre remains idyllic with its greens, church and blossom-decked trees in springtime.

Strange, weather-sculpted rocks at Plompton

West of the Ure

RIDE 36
NORTH YORKSHIRE
SE315712

This is a modestly undulating ride in the well-wooded area west of Ripon; a circuit never more than 7 miles (11km) from the city at any point. Mostly on quieter roads, it provides extensive panoramas, finishing with a good – if sometimes stony – descent. Much of the ride is within the Nidderdale Area of Outstanding Natural Beauty.

INFORMATION

Total Distance
20 miles (32km),
with about ½ mile (1km)
off-road.

Grade
2

OS Map
Landranger 1:50,000 sheet 99
(Northallerton & Ripon)

Tourist Information
Ripon (summer only),
tel: 01765 604625

Cycle Shops
John Donoghue, Ripon,
tel: 01765 601395;
Blossomgate Cycles, Ripon,
tel: 01765 606868

Nearest Railway Station
Thirsk (10 miles/16km);
Harrogate/Knaresborough
(11 miles/17.5km)

Refreshments
Cafés, restaurants and pubs are
plentiful in Ripon;
on the route there is a pub
at Galphay, two at
Kirkby Malzeard plus
a fish and chip shop;
restaurant, café and toilets at
the Fountains Abbey
Visitor Centre

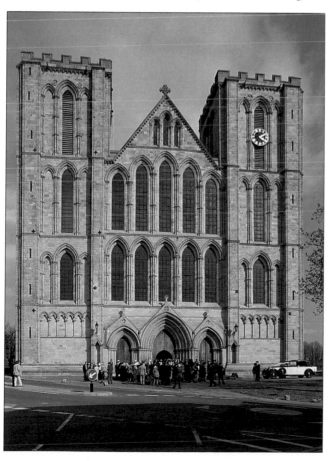

The splendid west front of Ripon Cathedral

START & ROUTE DIRECTIONS

Start

Ripon is on the A61 between Thirsk and Harrogate, some 5 miles (8km) west of the A1. The ride begins near the west door of the Cathedral, opposite the Tourist Information Centre. The nearest car park is at St Marygate.

Directions

1 🚲 Descend Bedern Bank to the roundabout and take the third exit, to Skellgarths. Go straight on at the traffic lights into Somerset Row. Continue along Mallorie Park Drive to join the B6265 at a T-junction, towards Pateley Bridge. In ½ mile (1km) turn right at T-junction, signed 'Galphay'. Climb gently to Birkby Lodge, thendescend steeply to Galphay Mill. Continue to Galphay.

2 🚲 Go through the village, keeping right past The Galphay Inn, then turn right at the T-junction for Kirkby Malzeard. At the market cross in Kirkby Malzeard turn left into the village street and continue to the end of the village. Bear left and ride over the ridge to follow a sharp, winding descent to Laverton.

3 🚲 On entering the village, take the right turn over the bridge and climb to a T-junction. Turn left, signed 'Grantley'. At the next main junction turn right. After 1 mile (1.5km) turn left at the T-junction, signed 'Ripon' and go on to Low Grantley.

4 🚲 From Low Grantley, continue east on a wooded lane for ¾ mile (1km) then go left, signed to Winksley. Continue to a left hand bend, and turn right (no sign) onto a single track road. Climb to the junction with the B6265; turn left and immediately right to Aldfield. Continue straight on to Fountains Abbey, taking a left turn through the gate beyond Fountains Farm to the National Trust Visitor Centre and the main Abbey entrance.

5 🚲 If time allows, the whole estate can be explored by entering at Canal Gates and leaving at Fountains Bridge. From the Visitor Centre (Swanley Grange) follow Ripon signs to the obelisk and pass through a gate to St Mary's Church, Studley Royal. Wheel your cycle down the carriageway of the deer park to the junction, then turn right on a path to the lakeside. Admission to the Abbey is at Canal Gate. Cyclists are permitted to walk with bikes through the landscaped water- gardens to the Abbey

The remains at Fountain's Abbey are extensive

and Fountains Hall. Exit to Fountains Bridge. Otherwise, from the Visitor Centre, retrace the route to Aldfield Lane; turn left, descending a sharp left-hand bend to Fountains Bridge.

6 🚲 Cross the bridge and continue south on Fountains Lane for about 1 mile (1.5km). At How Hill, opposite the tower, turn left into Whitcliffe Lane. Descend on a narrow, winding, patched road for 1 mile (1.5km) to Morcar Grange, then carry on for ½ mile (1km) on a stretch of rough bridleway to next junction – walking may be wise. Keep left for a further

¾ mile (1km) to the junction with West Lane, and stay on Whitcliffe Lane for a further ½ mile (1km).

7 🚲 At the junction with Harrogate Road, turn left;

continue over the bridge, then turn right at traffic lights into Water Skellgate. Continue to the roundabout, taking the first exit for the Cathedral, Minster Road and the St Marygate car park.

Ripon, one of Britain's smallest cities, feels more like a market town

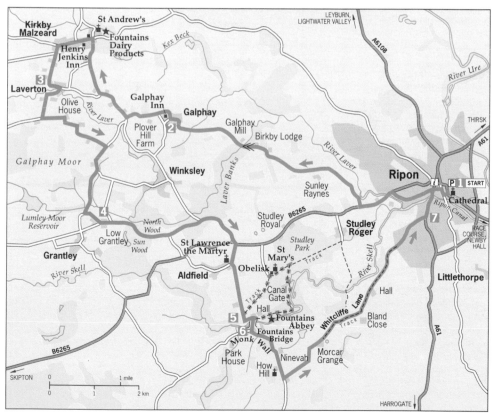

PLACES OF INTEREST

Ripon: One of Britain's smallest cities, dating back to 660AD, Ripon is dominated by a relatively small cathedral, built on the site of an earlier Saxon abbey. The cathedral is noted for its Early English decorated west front, a multiplicity of architectural styles and its lofty vaults.

The Thursday market is held in the large square surrounding Hawksmoor's 90ft (27m) 1702 obelisk. As a tourist base, the city is much visited and has the advantage of an attractive racecourse, the peaceful canal and Spa gardens, with the Lightwater Valley Theme Park and Newby Hall near at hand. The neighbouring villages of Sharow and Littlethorpe are also worth a visit.

Kirkby Malzeard: Once an important settlement, being granted a market charter in 1307 by Edward I, the village remains an attractive and vibrant centre. St Andrew's Church is on the site of a 10th-century church which, after a fire in 1908, was restored in 1910 through public subscription. On the eastern edge of the village is Fountains Dairy Products where Wensleydale cheese is produced.

Fountains Abbey: Now in the custody of the National Trust, along with the Studley Royal estate, the abbey is worth visiting for its picturesque setting in the secret wooded Skell valley. The buildings have been justly described as the most perfect monastic ruins in Europe,

Formal gardens at Studley Royal

and now hold World Heritage status. The medieval church with its magnificent tower is largely intact. Landscaped water-gardens in the narrow winding valley, along with the 17th-century Fountains Hall, add to the estate's attraction.

Aldfield: This hilltop hamlet has a small chapel-style church, which is dedicated to St Lawrence the Martyr. There is a quaint sundial over the porch, and the interior includes the original three-deck pulpit.

How Hill: The Monks Chapel at this elevated location is, unfortunately, not accessible because of restoration work. The structure was built in the 12th-century and may have been used for illicit gambling.

Studley Royal: The church of St Mary the Virgin is late 19th century with a tall spire and decorated chancel by William Burges. It is currently being restored by English Heritage. The Deer Park has a long carriage drive providing vehicular access to the church, and is aligned to give a clear view of Ripon Cathedral.

WHAT TO LOOK OUT FOR

On the road to Galphay, beside the River Laver watch for game birds in the meadows.
In Kirkby Malzeard note the market cross and its charter inscription, and the solid style of the stone houses with their mullioned windows. The Henry Jenkins inn sign pictures a village sword dancer who apparently lived to be 169.
The extensive Fountains Wall,
seen on the left after leaving Fountains Bridge is worthy of note.

RIDE 37
NORTH YORKSHIRE
SE112905

Leyburn and
Lower Wensleydale

This circuit in Lower Wensleydale is of an essentially hilly nature, but using largely quiet roads and lanes giving superb views, and with a historic, cultural theme. Note: many of the lanes on this route are extensively bordered by thorn hedges; at certain times of the year these are cut by flailing machines and debris may remain a hazard on the road.

INFORMATION

Total Distance
20 miles (32km)

Grade
3

OS Map
Landranger 1:50,000
sheet 99
(Northallerton & Ripon)

Tourist Information
Leyburn, tel: 01969 623069;
Bedale, tel: 01677 424604

Cycle Shop
G Dawkins, Bedale,
tel: 01677 422491

Nearest Railway Station
Northallerton (18 miles/29km);
Garsdale (24 miles/38.5 km)

Refreshments
Leyburn and Middleham offer a
selection of cafés and pubs.
Brymor Dairy at High Jervaulx serves
ice cream, and there is a tea room at
Jervaulx Abbey.
The Blue Lion at East Witton, The Old
Horn Inn at Spennithorne and
The Coverham Bridge Inn all serve
food. Pinker's Pond, between
Coverham and Middleham, is a good
place to picnic.
Toilets in Leyburn and Middleham

The view from No Man's Moor Lane

START & ROUTE DIRECTIONS

Start

Leyburn is situated on the A684, 12 miles (19km) west of the A1 Leeming Bar intersection and 36 miles (58km) east of junction 37 of the M6. The 130-space pay and display car park north of the market place is a good place to start the ride, but there is also parking elsewhere in the town. (*Note:* Leyburn has a large market on Fridays when pressure on space is greater, and approach roads may be busier.)

Directions

1️⃣ 🚲 From the market place follow the A684 east along Railway Street into Harmby Road, passing a craft/business park and an auction mart on the left. Young children may be able to use the footway for some distance. In 1 mile (1.5km) take the third turn right with care, after a scrap yard, into Colliwath Lane, signed 'Finghall'. Follow this lane, initially steep, then with a gradual descent to a T-junction. Turn left here and climb gradually. Keep straight ahead at the crossroads, and continue up the ridge to the route's high point of 574ft (175m), where the view eastwards includes the Cleveland Hills. Go straight on at further crossroads, and soon turn right, signed 'Newton le Willows'.

2️⃣ 🚲 Continue south-east on this undulating road, No Man's Moor Lane. Pass the water treatment works, and go up a short, steep hill – which may justify dismounting. At the summit

The busy market in Leyburn

crossroads, it is worth looking back to Thornton Reservoir where sailing dinghies can often be seen. Continue downhill to the next junction; go straight on for a short distance, then right at Cocked Hat Farm towards Jervaulx. This is Marriforth Lane which stays level for ¼ mile (0.5km) before dropping steeply to a crossroads. Go straight on to Kilgram Bridge.

3️⃣ 🚲 Cross the Ure and proceed along Kilgram Lane, climbing gradually to the junction with the A6108. (A short diversion towards High Jervaulx leads to the Brymor Dairy.)
Otherwise, the route continues west on the A6108, with Jervaulx Park on the right, to reach Jervaulx Abbey.

4️⃣ 🚲 From Jervaulx continue on the A6108, climbing

The map shows the route through Leyburn and Lower Wensleydale with labelled locations including Leyburn (START), Harmby, Constable Burton, Finghall, Spennithorpe, Middleham, East Witton, Jervaulx Abbey, and Coverham Bridge.

gently to East Witton. Pass the rugged, prominent church and keep left into the village, using the left side lane, bearing right at the top of village into Braithwaite Lane. This is a single track road so take care. (*Note:* for a short cut from East Witton, continue on the A6108, picking up the route at Ulshaw Bridge.) The lane climbs slightly, and in 1½ miles (2.5km) Braithwaite Hall can be seen on hillside to left. After a further ½ mile (1km) descend with care to the ancient Coverham Bridge. Go over the bridge, bearing left and then there is a sharp pull up to Coverham church.

5 🚲 At the junction, turn right towards Middleham, a moderate climb, then ride on the level passing Pinker's Pond. Ride over the moor to

Middleham to arrive in the upper square before exploring the castle. From the main square go east on the A6108 to Cover Bridge, turning left at the inn.

6 🚲 Go over Ulshaw Bridge and keep straight on, passing

At the crossroads, Kirkby Malzeard

the church on your right. Climb to a junction and turn left. Ride through Spennithorne, past the Hall and church, to turn left at the schoolhouse. Pass Thorney Hall and enter Harmby. Bearing right, the road climbs steeply to meet the A684. Turn left and re-trace the route back into Leyburn.

PLACES OF INTEREST

Leyburn: This pleasant old market town sits on a ledge, high on the north side of Wensleydale. The Shawl is a natural terrace extending for 2 miles (3km) on a rocky scar, and is associated with Mary, Queen of Scots.

Middleham: Dominated by its impressive castle, the town is centred round two squares, each with a cross, set on a steep slope. Views from the castle keep are extensive, and hours can be spent exploring the many rooms within this fortress, the 14th-century stronghold of the mighty Nevilles. On William's Hill, south of town, is the site of an earlier Norman motte and bailey. The church is largely 14th century with a defensive perpendicular tower. The town is renowned today for its racing stables.

Jervaulx Abbey: This privately owned Cistercian abbey dates back to 1156 and is open to the public. At the dissolution the abbey was more extensively dismantled than others, but a visit is never-theless fascinating, not least for its pastoral setting.

East Witton: The houses of this distinctive village face on to a central tree-lined green. At the east end is a tap, fixed to a glacial boulder. The church commemorates the 50th year of George III's reign.

Braithwaite Hall: This 17th-century manor house, with its three gables and mullioned windows, stands in particularly attractive countryside. A working farm, it is open by appointment.

Spennithorne: While Spennithorne Hall, with its Roman doric columns and bow windows, is impressive, remnants of the old hall can also be seen as you enter the village. The church of St Michael and All Angels has a fine 12th-century three-bay north arcade, and a curious wall painting of Father Time.

The ruins of Jervaulx Abbey stand in an attractive pastoral setting

Ulshaw Bridge: Dated 1674, and with three pairs of cutwaters, this is a magnificent bridge. Look out for the Roman Catholic church of St Simon and St Jude, almost hidden behind a Georgian house.

WHAT TO LOOK OUT FOR

Be sure to stop at Kilgram Bridge, a 15th-century structure with six arches and where sandpipers may be seen from April onwards. In Jervaulx Park look for the drumlins, rounded hillocks formed from glacial material during the Ice Age. Around Jervaulx Abbey itself, a variety of wild flowers common to a limestone habitat can be seen. Note also the stone embalming trough in the admission area. Through the Countryside Stewardship scheme, permitted access is available to a Brigantian fort above Braithwaite Hall – look for the small green-and-white map signs. On entering Middleham, note the unique Swine Cross in the upper square, as well as the ring formerly used for bull-baiting. At Ulshaw Bridge look for the dated sundial in one of the refuges and watch for swallows and sandmartins near the riversmeet from the end of May. In Harmby, there is a waterfall worth seeking out in the Gill, close to the A684.

RIDE 38
NORTH YORKSHIRE
SE613837

Helmsley and the Hambledon Hills

The route lies mostly at the western end of the Vale of Pickering, but also climbs over the eastern extremity of the Hambleton Hills with views over the Vale and the North York Moors beyond. The majority of the route is through quiet country lanes between hedgerows and mixed agricultural land. The route passes by Nunnington Hall, Gilling East model railway and Ampleforth Abbey and College.

INFORMATION

Total Distance
20½ miles (33km),
with 2½ miles (4km) off-road

Grade
3

OS Map
Landranger 1:50,000
sheet 100
(Malton & Pickering)

Tourist Information
Helmsley, tel: 01439 770173

Cycle Shop/Hire
Footloose (hire only), Helmsley,
tel: 01439 770886;
Strickland & Son,
Kirkbymoorside,
tel: 01751 431204

Nearest Railway Stations
Thirsk (15 miles/24km);
Malton (16 miles/25.5km)

Refreshments
There are numerous hotels, pubs and cafés in Helmsley.
Pubs on the route include The Star Inn at Harome (children welcome), The Royal Oak at Nunnington, The Fairfax Arms at Gilling East and The Malt Shovel Inn at Oswaldkirk.
There is a licensed restaurant at Duncombe Park and refreshments are available at Nunnington Hall.

The striking ruins of Helmsley Castle, destroyed in the Civil War

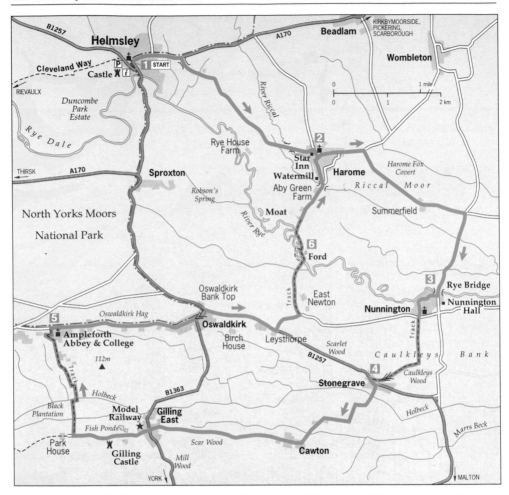

Ampleforth Abbey and College

START & ROUTE DIRECTIONS

Start

Helmsley lies 25 miles (40km) north of York, on the edge of the North York Moors National Park. The easiest access by car from the A1 and A19 trunk roads is via Thirsk along the A170. The starting point of the ride is on the market square outside the Town Hall, which houses the Tourist Information Office. (The long-stay car park in Helmsley is just west of the market place.)

Directions

1. ⬥ Proceed to the north-eastern corner of the market square (mini-roundabout) and ride eastwards on the A170 towards Scarborough. In ¾ mile (1km) turn right, signed 'Harome', over the old railway bridge, down into a dip and up the other side, then continue the steady descent into Harome.

2. ⬥ In the village bear right and then turn left, signed 'Wombleton'. Continue for ½ mile (1km) out of the village and fork right, signed 'Nunnington'. Continue for 1½ miles (2.5km) to the crossroads. Turn right here and after 1 mile (1.5km) reach Nunnington village.

3. ⬥ Immediately after the Rye Bridge turn right, and continue through the village. Climb the hill to the road junction by the church. Continue straight across and on to the bridleway. After ½ mile (1km) turn right through the gate, and continue to the fork in the track. Take the left fork through the gate, descend steeply and then go through another gate to reach the B1257 at Stonegrave.

4. ⬥ Turn sharp left onto the B1257 and shortlly turn right, signed 'Cawton'. Continue for 3 miles (5km) through Cawton to reach crossroads at Gilling. Go straight ahead over the B1363 into Pottergate.

Continue for ¾ mile (1km), ignoring the left fork. Turn right into the private road towards Ampleforth College (cyclists permitted). Continue on this road for 1¼ miles (2km), then bear left, uphill, past the Abbey and College buildings. On the north side of the buildings take the zig-zag road up to the public road.

5. ⬥ Turn right and continue, to reach Oswaldkirk in 1¾ miles (3km). Bear left up the steep hill on the B1363 to the T-junction with the B1257. Turn right towards Malton, and continue for ¾ mile (1km). Turn left, signed 'Nunnington'. In ⅓ mile (0.5km), where the road turns sharp right, turn left onto a bridleway. The sealed surface becomes a track, leading to the ford. Cross the River Rye and turn left, following the edge of the field and the river upstream.

(An alternative to crossing the ford is to walk the public footpath on the west bank of the river for 350yds (320m), to cross at the footbridge.)

6. ⬥ Continue on the edge of the field, with the River Rye on your left, to reach two wicket gates. Pass through them and continue with the fence and hedge on the right. Shortly, pass through a gate and on to a stone track which becomes a minor road at the first house. Continue for ½ mile (1km), go over a bridge and turn left at the junction. Continue for ⅓ mile (0.5km) to the road junction opposite Harome church. Turn left here, signed 'Helmsley', and retrace the route back to the market square and the start point of the ride.

Traditional stone-built cottages and a view through to the church, Helmsley

A perfect model at Nunnington Hall

PLACES OF INTEREST

Helmsley: An old market town with large market place built in traditional Yorkshire limestone and red pantile roofs with a simple market cross and memorial to the second Earl of Feversham. The castle (on the west side of the town) was slighted by the Parliamentary troops after the Royalist garrison surrendered in 1644. Duncombe Park Estate, home of the Earls of Feversham, lies south-west of the town. Dating from 1713, it was remodelled after a major fire in 1879. A girls' school for most of this century, it has now been restored to a superb family home. A 15th-century landscaped garden, Parkland Centre exhibition and country walks are among the attractions on offer.

Nunnington: The village of limestone buildings spreads up the hillside from the River Rye,

with a restored 13th-century church at its top. Nunnington Hall is a 17th-century house (NT), with panelled rooms and a magnificent staircase (open from April to October, not Mondays). It is reputed to be haunted.

Gilling East: Gilling Castle, formerly the residence of the Fairfax family, now a preparatory department for Ampleforth College, overlooks the village with its church and public house. In Pottergate, one of the

best model railways in Britain is to be found.

Ampleforth Abbey and College: This is one of the most famous Roman Catholic schools in Britain, with a museum and a library. The village was chosen as the site of the school in 1802 by English Benedictine monks who had fled from France to escape the French Revolution. There are magnificent views from the grounds towards Gilling Castle, 2 miles (3km) south. The church is relatively modern, completed in 1961.

WHAT TO LOOK OUT FOR

Sleepy Gilling East hides a number of surprises. Funds for the church clock, for example, were raised at celebrity cricket matches in 1889, organised by the great batsman, the Maharaja of Nawangar, Kumar Shri 'Ranji' Ranjitsinhji, who was staying at the Rectory – a munificent gesture by one of another faith.

RIDE 39
CUMBRIA
SD353981

Hawkshead and The Lakes

The ride takes in the lower hills of southern Cumbria, offering views of the high wild mountains, quiet cultivated valleys and fine examples of Lakeland farms and cottages. There are pleasantly demanding sections of rolling hills interspersed with level riding with the exception of two longer steep hills.

INFORMATION

Total Distance
21 miles (33.5km),
with 3 miles (5km) off-road

Grade
3

OS Map
Landranger 1:50,000 sheet 97
(Kendal to Morecambe)

Tourist Information
Hawkshead (summer only),
tel: 015394 36525;
Windermere,
tel: 015394 46499

Cycle Shops/Hire
Ghyllside Cycles, Ambleside,
tel: 015394 33592;
Grizedale Mountain Bikes,
tel: 01229 860369

Nearest Railway Station
Windermere

Refreshments
Hawkshead has many pubs
and cafés;
pubs on the route include
The Eagle's Head at Satterthwaite,
and there are tea rooms
at the Grizedale Forest
Visitor Centre.
Grizedale Forest offers
fine opportunities for picnicking

The village of Hawkshead is associated with both William Wordsworth and Beatrix Potter

Hanging baskets and colourful window boxes decorate The Queen's Head at Hawkshead

'Windermere', and again after 100yds (91m) cross the beck and turn left, signed 'Wray'.
Continue for 2 miles (3km), passing through the village of Colthouse to reach High Wray. In High Wray, turn right at the junction, signed 'Ferry & Unsuitable for Vehicles'.

2 ☍ Continue past Balla Wray Nursing Home, passing through the woods of Claife Estate. After 1½ undulating miles (2.5km), at Red Nab, go through the gate on to an unsurfaced road and ride along the lakeside, heading south. In 3 miles (5km) go over the cattle grid on to a tarmac road and eventually turn right onto the B5285.

3 ☍ After passing Ash Landing, climb the hill and immediately before the 'Far Sawrey' signpost turn left. Bear left again in a short distance, and descend to pass through High Cunsey. Follow this undulating lane for 2 miles (3km), bearing left at the fork in Low Cunsey; cross the stream and go over the hill to the T-junction opposite Graythwaite Hall.

4 ☍ Turn left here, and shortly right, signed 'Rusland'. Climb the hill and descend with care, then take the left fork to reach a junction by a telephone box, just after Crosslands Farm.

START & ROUTE DIRECTIONS

Start
The village of Hawkshead lies midway between Lake Windermere and Lake Coniston on the B5285. It is 4 miles (6.5km) from the Windermere car ferry. Begin the ride from the main car park in the centre of the

village, which has an information centre and public toilets.

Directions
1 ☍ Leave the car park, with the Tourist Information Office behind you on the left, and at the exit turn right, signed 'Windermere'. In 100yds (91m), at the T-junction turn left, signed

Turn right, signed 'Grizedale', and follow the lane between beech hedges and along the beck. Go straight on at the crossroads, climb the hill and after ½ mile (1km) turn left, signed 'Satterthwaite', and left again in a short distance. Continue past a picnic spot, to reach a T-junction opposite the post office at Force Mills.

5 🚲 Turn right here and enter Grizedale Forest Park, with the rapids of Force Mills on the left. After 1 mile (1.5km), enter Satterthwaite village, with The Eagle's Head pub on the left. Pass All Saints Church on the right and the village green on the left and continue, to reach Grizedale Hall and Visitor Centre. Continue for 3 miles (5km) past Grizedale Lodge Hotel to the top of the hill before descending to a T-junction. Turn left here to return to the centre of Hawkshead village and the start point of the ride.

Rhododendrons and azaleas flourish in the extensive landscaped gardens of Graythwaite Hall

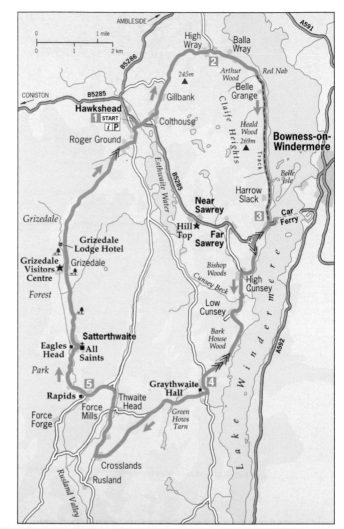

PLACES OF INTEREST

Hawkshead: The village was originally a Viking settlement and then an important centre under the control of Furness Abbey. It went into decline when bypassed by the railways. Now, with its attractive jumble of old and interesting buildings around courtyards and alleys, it is a busy and thriving centre.

The great Romantic poet William Wordsworth was educated at the Grammar School here. The Courthouse, formerly the Manor House, is owned by the National Trust and open to the public.

Hill Top (NT), the home of Beatrix Potter is just 2 miles (3km) away at Near Sawrey. She wrote and illustrated many of her 'Peter Rabbit' books in this 17th-century farmhouse, which contains her furniture and china.

Hawkshead, with Coniston Fells

Graythwaite Hall: This splendid Elizabethan hall is surrounded by 7 acres (3ha) of landscaped garden with shrubs, azaleas and rhododendrons (gardens are open to the public in season, but not the house).

Grizedale Forest Park and Hall (Forest Enterprises): This is the first Forestry Commission estate where special efforts were made to provide information for visitors. The centre illustrates the story of Grizedale, from its earliest state as a wild wood to its present role as an area managed for timber, wildlife and recreation.

Attractions at Grizedale include picnic sites, children's play area, off-road cycle trails, and sculpture and nature trails. There is also a unique theatre in the forest, presenting dance, drama and music events to suit all tastes throughout the year.

WHAT TO LOOK OUT FOR

This area was raided then settled by the Vikings and evidence of their occupation remains in placenames ending in 'thwaite', which in Norse means clearing.

Wild deer can be seen in Grizedale Forest, and there is rich birdlife in the area with many species of duck, and geese, green woodpeckers, tawny owls, snipe, buzzards and kingfishers.

Drumlins, egg-shaped landmarks of the Ice Age, can be seen in the Rusland Valley, which was once under water.

RIDE 40
CUMBRIA
NY682204

The Vale of Eden

The Eden Valley is a hilly area running from north to south between the Lake District mountains to the west and the long, high line of the Pennines to the east. It is a quiet, unspoiled area offering panoramic views, and contrasting lush farmland with wild upland scenery.

INFORMATION

Total Distance
27 miles
(43.5km)

Grade
3

Cherry blossom on the village green at Temple Sowerby

OS Map
Landranger 1:50,000 sheet 91
(Appleby-in-Westmorland)

Tourist Information
Appleby-in-Westmorland,
tel: 017683 51177

Cycle Shops/Hire
Appleby Cycle Hire,
tel: 01768 353533

Nearest Railway Station
Appleby-in-Westmorland

Refreshments
In Appleby there is a selection of pubs and cafés, and The Royal Oak Inn welcomes children. Along the route there are pubs at Dufton, Temple Sowerby, and Bolton, and one at Gullom Holme which offers a play area and children's meals

START & ROUTE DIRECTIONS

Start

Appleby-in-Westmorland lies just off the A66 some 13 miles (21km) south-east of Penrith and the M6 and 37 miles (59.5km) west of Scotch Corner on the A1. Begin the ride from the car park (pay and display) in Chapel Street some 200yds (185m) south-west of the church.

Directions

1️⃣ 🚲 Leave the car park by Low Wiend, immediately opposite the entrance; join Boroughgate in front of the cloisters, and bear left into Bridge Street to cross the Eden Bridge. At the T-junction turn right signed 'Brough'.

Continue up the hill and after 300yds (270m) turn left into Drawbriggs Lane signed 'Hilton and Murton'. Follow this road as it bends to the right under the railway bridge. At the junction just beyond the cheese factory turn left. Ignoring all side roads, follow this undulating road signed 'Hilton and Murton' for 3½ miles (5.5km), going under the A66, passing by the farms of Kirkber and Langton, and following Hilton Beck into Hilton.

2️⃣ 🚲 Passing by Hilton, follow the road to the left and continue along the fellside. This is the highest point of the route, with High Cup

Cottages at Milburn

Nick to the right. In 3½ miles (5.5km) turn right and proceed into Dufton.

3️⃣ 🚲 Leave Dufton, ignoring the side road on the left. Continue down the hill and after 1½ miles (2.5km) pass through the village of Knock. Ignoring lanes left and right, proceed for 2 miles (3km), passing through Silverband to reach a T-junction. Turn right, signed 'Milburn'. Pass The Stag Inn and continue for a further ½ mile (1km) to bear right into Milburn. Leave the village from the bottom of the green, signposted to Newbiggin. In 100yds (91m) bear left, signposted to Newbiggin and Temple Sowerby, and shortly bear right, signed 'Newbiggin'.

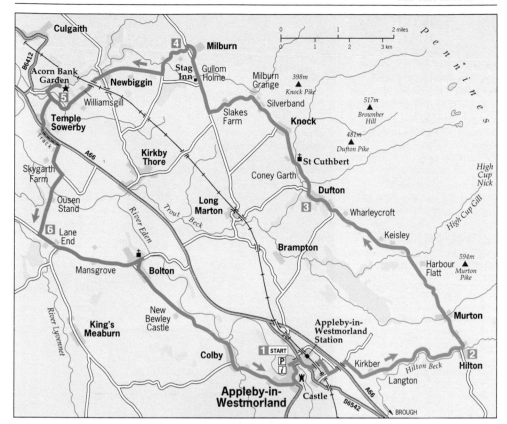

4 In 1 mile (1.5km) turn right signed 'Newbiggin', follow this road for 2 miles (3km), passing the crossroads in Newbiggin and the left turn to Temple Sowerby, to reach Acorn Bank House and Gardens on the right.

5 Retrace the route and turn right towards Temple Sowerby. Pass through the village and dismount to cross the A66. Turn left to follow the footpath for 350yds (320m), then remount and turn right into a lane, signed 'Morland'. In ½ mile (1km) turn right, signed to Cliburn and Morland. Cross the River Eden and continue to a T-junction. Turn left here, signed to Morland and Bolton.

6 In 2 miles (3km) enter the village of Bolton, and keep left to visit the church. Return to the junction and turn left past the post office, then shortly left again, and follow this undulating road along the riverside through Colby back to Appleby. At the T-junction turn left, then bear immediately right and climb the hill to High Cross. Go down the hill, turn left before the post office, then first right back to the car park.

The unusual fountain on the village green at Dufton

PLACES OF INTEREST

Appleby: This quiet historic town, set on a sheltered bend of the River Eden, was for 800 years the county town of Westmorland. A fine wide main street, Boroughgate, runs up from St Lawrence's Church and Low Cross to High Cross and the Norman castle, with its fine Keep and great hall. Clifford family paintings and some items of the Nanking Cargo are displayed in the castle (open from April to October). The Rare Breeds Survival Trust maintains a collection of unusual birds and animals in the castle grounds. Also note the ancient two-storied Moot Hall, alms houses, riverside walks and nature trail, steam trains, and the famous Horse Fair in June.

East Fellside Villages: Along this side of the Pennine range there are many quiet villages such as Hilton, Dufton and Milburn. They have spacious central greens bordered by squat 18th-century sandstone houses. St Cuthbert's Church, Dufton, is shared with Knock and stands by its 1785 rectory between the villages. It retains elegant brass numbers for each pew, and set into the west end of the south aisle is a weathered stone with fine Saxon carvings of the symbols of the bow, arrow and axe.

Acorn Bank Garden, Temple Sowerby: Once the Manor House for Temple Sowerby and owned by the Knights Templar, it is now a Sue Ryder Home and owned by the National Trust. The small but delightful garden of some 2½ acres

(1ha) has a particularly interesting walled herb garden, with an extensive collection of over 180 varieties of medicinal

Almshouses at Appleby

and culinary herbs (garden only open from April to October).

WHAT TO LOOK OUT FOR

A wide variety of birds including heron, buzzard, kestrel and small hedgerow species may be seen.
Conical hills, separated from the main Pennine chain during geological disturbance, are found behind Murton, Dufton and Knock. The route also passes close to High Cup Nick, an extraordinary cleft in the hills between Hilton and Dufton which is visible from many points of the ride.

Beadnell, Bamburgh and Craster

RIDE 41
NORTHUMBERLAND
NU235287

This ride sets out along a beautiful stretch of the Northumberland coast, taking in the popular resort of Seahouses and the village of Bamburgh with its dramatic castle. The return route leaves the coast to explore a network of byroads through rural country-side before returning to the sea again at Craster.

INFORMATION

Total Distance
32 miles (51km)

Grade
1

OS Map
Landranger 1:50,000 sheets 75
(Berwick-upon-Tweed) and 81
(Alnwick & Morpeth)

Cycle Shops/Hire
Breeze's Bikes, Amble,
tel: 01665 710323

Tourist Information
Craster (summer only),
tel: 01665 576007; Berwick-upon-
Tweed, tel: 01289 330733

Nearest Railway Station
Chathill (on route)

Refreshments
Various pubs, restaurants and
cafés in Seahouses, including
The Olde Ships;
cafés in Craster, in Bamburgh
and at Bamburgh Castle;
The Jolly Fisherman at Craster is a
popular family pub

Lobster pots at Craster

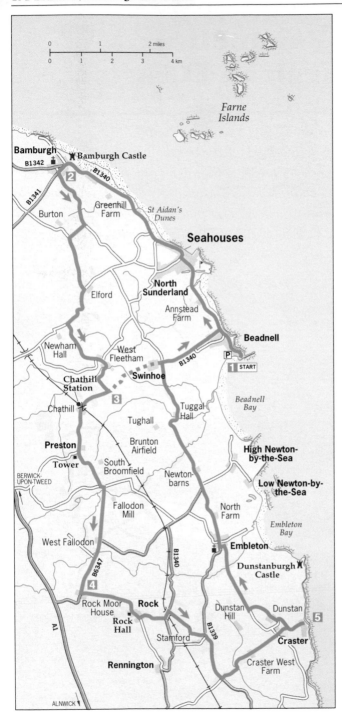

Start
Beadnell lies on the
Northumberland coast
between Seahouses and
Craster, on the B1340.
Park down at Beadnell
Harbour.

Directions
1 ⚲ Follow the road back
up from Beadnell Harbour to
Beadnell village and fork
right on to the B1340,
heading north. Continue
beside the dunes for 2 miles
(3km) to reach Seahouses.
Follow the B1340 right along
the main street of Seahouses.
At the harbour, fork left and
follow the coast road for a
further 3 miles (5km) to
Bamburgh, with views to
the right across to the Farne
Islands.

2 ⚲ Bear left in front of the
great castle, along the main
street of Bamburgh. At the
top of the main street, fork left
and then turn left on to a
narrow road, heading
southwards. In 1½ miles
(2.5km), turn right and ½
mile (1km) further turn left.
Continue, to reach a
T-junction in Elford. Turn
right here, and in 1 mile
(1.5km) turn left. Stay on
this road, to pass through
West Fleetham. Continue for
½ mile (1km) to reach a
T-junction.

3 ⚲ Turn left here for a
short-cut back to Beadnell.
Otherwise, turn right, cross
over the railway by Chathill
Station, then continue for
just over a mile to reach

Preston, passing the old tower on the right. Bear left through Preston, then in 1 mile (1.5km) turn left and immediately right. In 1 mile (1.5km) bear right on to the B6347 and after a further mile turn left on to a narrow lane towards Rock.

4 🚲 Continue through Rock and turn left; after ½ mile (1km) turn left on to the B1340. Cross a railway bridge and immediately turn right towards Stamford. Continue, to meet the B1339; turn right here, and in about a mile turn left on to a minor road towards Craster. Stay on this road into Craster, and keep straight on to the little harbour.

5 🚲 Retrace the route through Craster for a short distance and fork right to pass through Dunstan. Beyond Dunstan turn right at a T-junction and continue for 1½ miles (2.5km) to Embleton, passing Dunstanburgh Castle on the right. At Embleton church turn right on to the B1339 and continue on this road towards Bamburgh. Pass a turning to the right to the peaceful twin villages of High Newton and Low Newton-by-the-Sea, and continue for 3½ miles (5.5km) to Swinhoe. Follow the road right here and continue into Beadnell. At the coast where the B1340 bears left, turn right and return to the harbour.

The shell of the huge castle at Bamburgh successfully dominates this stretch of coastline

PLACES OF INTEREST

Beadnell: This pleasant small fishing village and coastal resort lies to the north of Beadnell Bay with its sandy beach. At the side of the little harbour which is used by both fishermen and fair-weather sailors, there are some late 18th-century lime kilns which are preserved by the National Trust.

Seahouses: Once a peaceful village, Seahouses is now a thriving holiday centre, and the main point for day trips to visit the seabird colonies and other wildlife of the Farne Islands. St Aidan's Dunes, to the north of Seahouses, is an area cared for by the National Trust.

The remains of lime kilns, dating from the 18th century, at Beadell

Bamburgh: You can hardly miss the huge castle which dominates this little village. Built in Norman times and heavily restored and altered in the 18th and 19th centuries, it has served as fort, royal residence, training centre for domestic staff and site of a corn mill for the benefit of the poor.
At the top of the main village street is a small museum housing relics of Grace Darling, the heroine of a dramatic sea rescue in 1838. The prime exhibit is the actual cobble used in the rescue of the crew

of the SS *Forfarshire*. Grace Darling is buried in the churchyard of St Aidan's.

Rock: The old manor house of Rock Hall was built on the site of a 15th-century pele tower, and from 1804 was the seat of the Bosanquet family. It served as a Youth Hostel from 1950–91.
The approach to the Hall, now private property, is along a lane lined with picturesque cottages, and there is a small but beautiful church.

Craster: On the right as you approach Craster there is a gateway and Craster Tower. Craster is a delightful fishing village with a tiny harbour, best known for its famous oak-smoked kippers. The harbour was the unusual bequest of the Craster family (owners of Craster Tower) in 1906, in memory of a family member who died on active service in Tibet. Fishing boats still bring in crab and lobster; once the traffic was the local basaltic rock known as whinstone. There is a shell museum.
On either side of the village is unspoiled and majestic cliff scenery, but to see the best of it involves a walk. One of the most popular walks from Craster is to the ruins of the 16th-century Dunstanburgh Castle. This looks out over the sea and has associations with the Wars of the Roses. It is a 2 mile (3km) return walk from Craster.

WHAT TO LOOK OUT FOR

The jagged ruin of Dunstanburgh Castle is clearly visible on the coast, and a pleasant walk leads here from Craster. The castle was built in 1316 by Thomas, Earl of Lancaster, and later enlarged by John of Gaunt.
In ruins since Tudor times, its skeletal profile and spectacular clifftop location have made it a favourite subject for artists over the centuries – Turner painted it three times.

Highlights of Cycling History by Thornhill

This ride passes through beautiful mid-Nithsdale and is mainly on very quiet, well surfaced roads. It takes in the place where the world's first pedal bicycle was conceived, as well as the Scottish Museum of Cycling. There are also two splendid castles belonging to the Dukes of Buccleuch and Queensberry.

RIDE 42
DUMFRIES & GALLOWAY
NX878955

INFORMATION

Distance
20 miles (32km),
with 2 miles (3km) off-road

Grade
Generally 2, but with
three significant hills

OS Map
Landranger 1:50,000 sheet 78
(Nithsdale & Annandale)

Tourist Information
Dumfries,
tel: 01387 253862

Cycle Shop/Hire
Andy Barr, Drumlanrig,
tel: 01848 330325

Nearest Railway Stations
Dumfries (14 miles/22.5km, or,
19 miles/30.5km by KM Trail);
Sanquhar (12 miles/20km)

Refreshments
Pubs and cafés at Thornhill welcome
children, there is a pub at
Penpont,
and a café serves summer teas at
Drumlanrig Castle;
excellent picnic spots around
Morton Castle and Loch

The high walls of ruined Morton Castle

START & ROUTE DIRECTIONS

Start

Thornhill lies on the A76 Dumfries to Kilmarnock road, 14 miles (22.5km) north of Dumfries. Its streets are so wide that it is one of the few places in the country without parking restrictions.

Directions

1 🚲 From the cross at the centre of Thornhill, go north and turn left into New Street. Continue down the steep hill, and go straight ahead at the crossroads at the bottom. Continue over the bridge across the normally peaceful River Nith, popular with fishermen, and turn first left. Stay on this level road for 1½ miles (2.5km). After the metal bridge and short uphill stretch, stop at the first houses of Keir Mill and take your bike along the path on the left to the cemetery. At the bottom of the cemetery is the grey-painted gravestone of Kirkpatrick Macmillan, the 'Father of the Bicycle'. Return to the road.

2 🚲 Continue through Keir, and at the T-junction turn right. In a short distance on the left you will pass Courthill Smithy. Continue for 1 mile (1.5km) to Penpont, and turn right at the crossroads. At the next hamlet, Burnhead, take the left fork (through the 30mph zone), and continue straight on for nearly 2 miles (3km) to cross a cattle grid. Shortly after that, bear left (cyclists ignore the 'No entry' signs) up a steep hill, passing on your left the flat area that was a Roman camp and where the KM Cycle Rally is held, to Drumlanrig Castle.

3 🚲 Leave Drumlanrig along the straight lime avenue, and continue downhill into the Nith gorge. Turn left over the bridge, continue up the hill to fork right, and cross the A76 with care (signposted 'Durisdeer'). To see a grove of the massive Wellingtonia trees, take the second track on your left by the cottages, climbing steeply at first; fork right once and left twice and return. Otherwise, continue for nearly a mile to a staggered crossroads at the A702 (no sign). Go straight across this, over the railway line, and straight on at the next crossroads (no sign), rising all the time. In nearly 1 mile (1.5km) take the track left to Morton Castle and Loch (sign on the gate 'Morton Castle Loch').

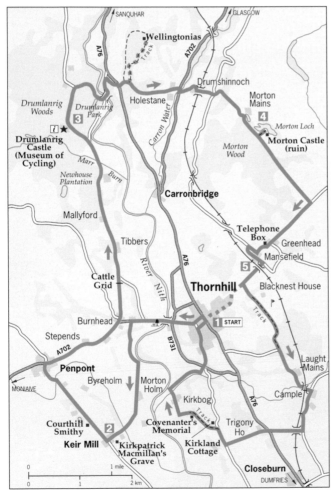

4 🚲 Return to the road and turn left (rather uneven) and continue to the T-junction. Turn right, descending the biggest downhill of the route. Keep straight on past a phone box and follow the road round a right-hand bend. At the next junction turn very sharp left. In ½ mile (1km) turn sharply right, down under the railway. (For a short cut, continue straight along this road to return to the centre of Thornhill.)

5 🚲 Shortly after the railway, turn left on to the track, which starts tarred, through the golf course. When you reach the public road, go straight on to the next hamlet, Cample, and turn right just after the railway bridge. Turn next right, cross the A76 carefully and at the next junction (made to look like a crossroads by a track) turn right. In a short distance turn left at Kirkland Cottage on to a track, and continue down past a cemetery (Old Dalgarnock Covenanters'

The cycle museum at Drumlanrig is well worth exploring

Memorial); please shut the gates. Follow the track to the next public road, and continue across a staggered junction to return to Thornhill.

The castle at Drumlanrig was built by the Duke of Queensberry

PLACES OF INTEREST

The 'Father of the Bicycle':
Kirkpatrick Macmillan built the world's first pedal bicycle in his smithy at Courthill in 1839. His achievements are commemorated on the gravestone at Keir, where he and his family lie. At the smithy, three plaques have been erected over the years. As is often the case, the significance of Macmillan's invention was not fully appreciated until after his death. A replica of his bicycle is at the Cycle Museum at Drumlanrig, which houses a fine collection tracing the history of cycling. The 'KM Trail' signs that you see mark the quiet cycle route from Dumfries to Keir and Drumlanrig in memory of the father of the modern bicycle.

Drumlanrig Castle: The unusual pink sandstone palace of Drumlanrig was built in the later 17th century, but the first Duke of Queensberry, who had built the castle's, lived in it for only one day. Prince Charles Edward Stuart also stayed for only one night in 1745. In 1810 it passed to the Dukes of Buccleuch, and many of their family treasures are displayed here. The castle is also a Mecca for cyclists, with the Scottish Museum of Cycling, and trails laid out through the magnificent parkland. There is also an annual cyclists' rally, held around May. (Castle and grounds are open from May to August, but the castle is closed on Thursdays).

Morton Castle: This substantial, picturesque ruin is set on a headland, partly surrounded by a kidney-shaped loch. Little is know about its history, but it was probably built by the Douglases, and was abandoned in the 18th century by their heirs, the Dukes of Queensberry and Buccleuch. It makes an excellent place to stop for a picnic.

The mercat cross, Thornhill

WHAT TO LOOK OUT FOR

Among the many venerable trees particularly around Drumlanrig, look out for the biggest sycamore in Britain, and the statistics that are on its sign. Most of the giant firs in the area are Douglas fir, but the really tall firs with the soft bark are Wellingtonias.

'CT' signs along the route mark gravestones and memorials of the Covenanters, a group of people who objected to the interference of the monarchy in affairs of religion, and who feared the rise of Catholicism. The National Covenant of 1638 marked their emergence as a serious political force; compelled to leave the Church, they continued to preach and worship in conventicles, one of which was at Crichope Linn. Ruthlessly persecuted by the Crown, as many as 18,000 died between 1661–88, in a particularly bitter phase of the history of the Church in Scotland.

A Circuit East of Edinburgh

INFORMATION

Distance
15 miles (24km),
with 7 miles (11.5km)
off-road

Grade
2

OS Map
Landranger 1:50,000
sheet 66
(Edinburgh & Midlothian)

Tourist Information
Musselburgh (summer only),
tel: 0131 665 6597;
Granada Service Area off A1,

There are fine views of the Pentland and Lammermuir Hills as you travel the quiet roads and cycle paths of this fairly gentle route there are only two short sections on main roads). Points of interest include the Inveresk Lodge Garden, Preston Tower and the Prestongrange Industrial Museum.

Old Craighall
near Musselburgh,
tel: 0131 653 6172

Cycle Shops/Hire
The New Bike Shop (hire),
Tollcross, Edinburgh,
tel: 0131 228 6333

Refreshments
Pubs and cafés in
Musselburgh,
including Luca's Café;
The Quayside Restaurant, Fisherrow;
summer teas and snacks
at the Prestongrange Industrial
Heritage Museum

The River Esk flows through Musselburgh into the Firth of Forth

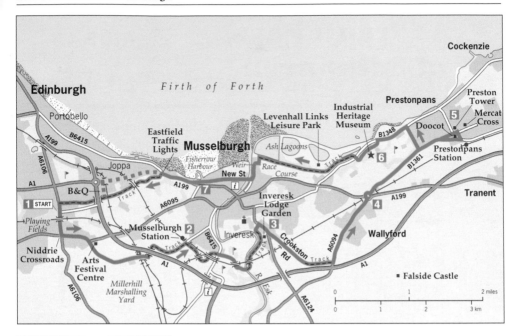

Start
The ride starts at the Jewel
playing fields at the junction
of Duddingston Park South
and the Jewel, 4 miles (6.5km)
to the east of Edinburgh.
Park carefully at the side of
the road. The Innocent
Cycle Path runs direct to this
point from the Royal
Commonwealth Pool in
central Edinburgh, 2½ miles
(4km) away.

Directions
① ⑯ From the Jewel Playing
Fields head south along
Duddingston Park South.
Pass under the railway
bridge, and at the traffic lights
at Niddrie Crossroads turn
left. Turn right at the old
church that is now the
Craigmillar Arts Festival
Centre on to Whitehill Road.

Continue for 1 mile (1.5km),
cross the railway at Millerhill
Depot and then turn left on to
the cycle path. Pass under the
A1 by the subway and
immediately turn right
following the sign 'Fisherrow
and Musselburgh Station';
continue to the station via the
cycle gate.

② ⑯ By Musselburgh Station
turn right on to the path
signposted 'Monktonhall and
River Esk Walkway'. After
½ mile (1km) pass through
the railway tunnel and follow
the path to the left for a short
distance. Pass through a
second railway tunnel and
enter the Stoneybank
Housing Estate, where you
turn right, left and right to
come out at the mini-
roundabout on the B6415.
Go straight on to Ferguson
Drive, passing the Monktohall
Golf Clubhouse on your left.

The road goes under the
railway (bridge 27) and
brings you to a footbridge
over the River Esk. Cross the
river and turn left along the
track towards Inveresk and
Musselburgh. After 1 mile
(1.5km) turn right away from
the river and go up the short
hill into Inveresk. Turn right
at the main road and pass
Inveresk Lodge Garden on
the right.

③ ⑯ Continue through
Inveresk village; bear left at
Crookston Road and go on to
cross over the railway bridge
(cycles and pedestrians only).
This road eventually becomes
a cycle path alongside the A1,
for ½ mile (1km). On this
section you should get a fine
view of the white-painted
Falside Castle, on the skyline
ahead. At the junction with
the A6094 turn left and head
into Wallyford. On the far side

of the village take the second exit on the roundabout, the B1361 to North Berwick.

4 🚲 Continue along the B1361 for 1½ miles (2.5km) to Prestonpans, and stay on the North Berwick Road until you come to the Doocot (dovecot) on the left. Turn left just after this and follow signs to Preston Tower and Garden, looking out for the fine Mercat Cross. The gardens at Preston Tower make an ideal picnic stop. (If you have time, you may like to visit the battle site of the 1745 Battle of Prestonpans, which is another mile along the North Berwick Road.)

5 🚲 From Preston Tower head back towards Edinburgh on the B1361 and turn right at the outskirts of Prestonpans along Prestongrange Road. On a clear day you will be able to see the twin peaks of East and West Lomond, and the three high-rise apartment blocks across the Forth at Kirkcaldy. At the coast road, the B1348, turn left and continue to the Prestongrange Industrial Heritage Museum.

6 🚲 Stay on this road, and just after joining the main road (B1348) cross over on to the track at the entrance to the Levenhall Links Leisure Park. Follow this behind the houses and then between the race course and the Ash Lagoons. Stay beside the race course, and turn left by the boulders into the Goose Green housing scheme. Take the first turn on the right, to come out at the weir on the River Esk. You will see the footbridge to your left: cross this and carry straight on along New Street. Continue to Fisherrow Harbour, where you can buy fresh fish and stop for refreshment.

Crossing the River Esk

7 🚲 At the end of New Street join the A199 heading towards Edinburgh. Go straight on, and at the traffic lights at Eastfield bear left. At this point, look for the new cycle path leading off to the left (completion is due in autumn 1995) which will return you to your starting point at the Jewel.
If you prefer to stay on the road continue for a mile to the roundabout at the A1 where you should take the pavement on the left (this is dual use for cyclists and pedestrians); follow the cycle/walkway, passing B&Q and its car park before taking the subway under the A1. Stay on the cycle path between the houses and the Niddrie Burn to return to the starting point at the Jewel.

PLACES OF INTEREST

Inveresk: This charming village is now properly a suburb of Musselburgh, but nevertheless retains its own distinctive character. Extensive Roman remains have been found here, but it is the Georgian period which has left its mark on the village, with pleasing houses and an elegant church. Inveresk Lodge Gardens (NTS) specialises in plants for growing in smaller gardens, and is well worth a visit (open daily, all year).

Prestongrange Industrial Heritage Museum: The site, the oldest documented coal mine in Britain, is dominated by the Giant Beam Engine, which was originally used to pump out mine workings and was in use until 1954. The main exhibits are out of doors and can be viewed when the museum is closed (open from April to September).

Prestonpans: Prestonpans gained its name from the salt pans, constructed here in the 12th century by monks from Newbattle Abbey. Its most famous feature is the elaborate Mercat Cross, which dates from 1617 – a golden sandstone rotunda topped by a tall pillar, and with a unicorn on top of that. Preston Tower is now a ruin: built in the 15th century, it was burned down several times (once by Cromwell) before its owners, the Hamiltons of

Passing pantiled cottages, Fisherrow

Preston, moved out to more convenient accommodation.

Musselburgh: As the harbour suggests, fishing was the main industry of this town, which is named after a mussel bed at the river mouth. A chapel and hermitage here became a popular site of pilgrimage in the early 16th century but were destroyed, along with the rest of the town, in 1544.

WHAT TO LOOK OUT FOR

Fisherrow developed independently of Musselburgh and it had strong trading links with the Netherlands in the 15th century. Look out for a Flemish influence in some of the older buildings of Fisherrow.
There are many freshwater wild flowers along the River Esk Cycle/Walkway, especially in May and June, and you will often see swans here too.
Levenhall Links Leisure Park hosts a good collection of ducks, geese and marsh birds. Also look out for seaside plants such as viper's bugloss, common rock rose and thrift.

Benderloch, Loch Creran and Loch Etive

This is a ride to give you a taste of the Scottish west coast and sea loch scenery, and is almost entirely on well surfaced minor roads. The route is mainly gently undulating except for a short climb through the forest; but the rewards for that are superb views of Loch Etive plus a fine descent. You might even glimpse a golden eagle in this area.

RIDE 44
STRATHCLYDE
NM905380

INFORMATION

Distance
17 miles (27.5km)

Grade
2

OS Map
Landranger 1:50,000 sheet 49
(Oban & East Mull)

Tourist Information
Oban, tel: 01631 563122

Cycle Shop/Hire
Oban Cycles,
tel: 01631 566996

Nearest Railway Station
Connel (2 miles/3km);
Oban (7 miles/11km)

Refreshments
There are cafés at Benderloch
and Argyll Pottery,
and a restaurant and coffee shop at
the Sea Life Centre;
refreshments are also available
to visitors to Ardchattan
Priory Garden

*Gorse blossoms in front of the old
tower house of Barcaldine Castle*

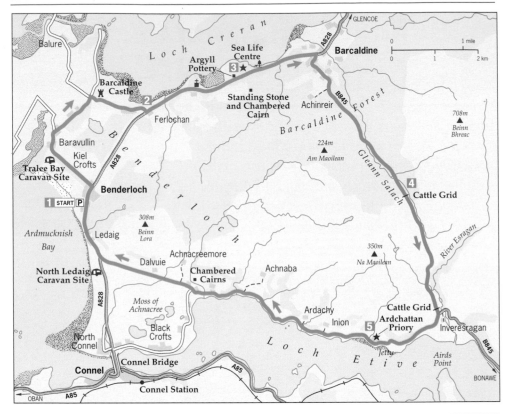

The view across Loch Etive to Ben Cruachan from Ardchattan point

START & ROUTE DIRECTIONS

Start

Benderloch village lies 7 miles (11km) north of Oban, and 2 miles (3km) north of Connel Bridge on the A828 from its junction with the A85. Begin the ride at the car park on the left of the A828, at the phone box opposite the petrol station.

Directions

1 🚲 Turn left on leaving the car park, heading north, and in ½ mile (1km) bear left on to minor road signed 'South Shian'. Follow this road, passing Tralee Bay caravan site and craft studio. Follow

this road, keeping right, and at the crossroads turn right. Go uphill, and Barcaldine Castle is on your left. Continue, to meet the main road (A828) at a T-junction.

2 🚲 Turn left here, and continue for 2½ miles (4km), to pass the Argyll Pottery (you can see the potters at work). Shortly after this, reach the Sea Life Centre on your left.

3 🚲 Continue on the A828 to a main junction in Barcaldine. Turn right on to the B845, signposted to Bonawe. This is a narrow

Benrderloch, the start of the ride, lies to the north of Connel Bridge

road with passing places, which climbs steadily through Barcaldine Forest, offering plenty of potential picnic sites beside the burn. The road levels off, and just before descending there is a cattle grid.

4 🚲 The descent from here is steep, with superb views of Loch Etive and the adjoining hills. Beware of a second cattle grid at the bottom of the slope. Where the main road leads sharply left, turn right, signposted to North Connel. Continue along Loch

Etiveside, past a shingle beach and jetty, to reach Ardchattan Priory. The entrance to the Priory is at the far end of the wall, to the right.

5 🚲 Continue along the road which hugs the shore of the loch, until you climb gently away from the water and reach a junction. Keep straight on (do not go to North Connel) along this minor road for 1½ miles (2.5km) to reach a junction with the A828, opposite North Ledaig caravan site. Turn right and continue to Benderloch, to return to the car park.

PLACES OF INTEREST

Barcaldine Castle: A castle was built here, on the south shore of Loch Creran, in 1609 by Campbell of Glenorchy. It is notorious as the place where MacIan of Glencoe was forced to shelter from blizzards, on his way to take the oath of allegiance at Inverary: he arrived too late, and the resulting disputes led to the dreadful Massacre of Glencoe. Deserted in the 18th century, the castle was restored at the turn of the century, and is privately owned.

Sea Life Centre: In a beautiful location on the sea loch, this is a marvellous place to view the underwater life of Britain's coastline – without getting your feet wet. There is a touch tank,

The ruins of Ardchattan Priory

and in summer you may see young seals awaiting release back into the wild. With daily talks and feeding demonstrations, there's always something going on here. (Open all year, but weekends only in December and January.)

Ardchattan Priory: The old granite house of Ardchattan began its existence in the 13th century, when a priory and church were built here for the French Valliscaulian order. Significantly enlarged at the end of the 15th century, the priory later changed hands and part of the house became a family residence. Ancient carved tombstones can still be seen in the remains of the choir and transepts. There is also an attractive garden at Ardchattan (open from Easter to October; Priory by appointment only).

WHAT TO LOOK OUT FOR

This part of Argyll has been occupied since earliest times, and the ride takes you past a number of burial chambers and standing stones. At Benderloch, near the railway station and on the shores of the bay, a low twin-peaked hill is crowned by the remains of a vitrified fort. On the hillside opposite the Sea Life Centre is a standing stone, with a cairn nearby, and as you leave the shores of Loch Etive, there are chambered cairns on the slopes to your right.

Aberfeldy, Fortingall and Loch Tay

This is a ride which explores part of central Perthshire which, geologically, is on the edge of the Highlands. The boundary line goes from Helensburgh in the west to Stonehaven on the east coast. Perthshire shows the change from the Lowlands dramatically, with its narrow valleys, lochs and high mountains providing a microcosm of some of Scotland's finest scenery.

RIDE 45
CENTRAL
NN852492

INFORMATION

Distance
24 miles (38.5km)

Grade
2

OS Map
Landranger 1:50,000 sheet 52
(Pitlochry to Crieff)

Tourist Information
Aberfeldy, tel: 01887 820276

Cycle Hire
Dunolly House, Aberfeldy,
tel: 01887 820298

Nearest Railway Station
Pitlochry (14 miles/22.5km)

Refreshments
There are pubs, cafés and public
toilets in Aberfeldy;
tea rooms and toilets at
Castle Menzies;
hotels offering refreshment all
along the route.
Good picnic spots beside
Loch Tay

The village of Kenmore, viewed from across the loch

START & ROUTE DIRECTIONS

Start

Aberfeldy lies about 14 miles (22.5km) south-west of Pitlochry, on the banks of the River Tay at the junction of the A827 and the A826. There are a number of small free car parks, although some are limited waiting. The recommended parking for this ride is at the riverside Taybridge Drive (no restrictions), on the left of the B846 just before Wade's Bridge and next to the Black Watch Memorial, which commemorates the enrolling of this famous old Scottish regiment in 1739.

Directions

1 🚲 Leave Taybridge Drive, cross Wade's Bridge and continue along the B846, passing the historic Weem Hotel on your right. Almost immediately after this on your right is the entrance drive to Castle Menzies. Continue on the B846 to pass Farleyer House (restaurant). Continue on this road for about 3 miles (5km), passing stone circles on the left, and a turning signed 'Kenmore', to turn left at the Coshieville Hotel, signposted to Fortingall, Glen Lyon and Fearnan.

2 🚲 Continue on this road towards Fortingall, passing the site of an ancient fort on a hill, right, after about 2 miles (3km). Cycle through Fortingall, and just beyond the village turn right to enter the beautiful valley of Glen Lyon. It is well worth a detour as far as the steep hill on your right, known as Macgregor's Leap; return to the main route and turn right, towards Fearnan.

3 🚲 Continue on this road to descend to Fearnan, on the shores of Loch Tay – the descent is steep, so be careful. As you reach Fearnan, bear right towards Killin, and shortly come to a T-junction, facing the loch.

Wade's Bridge over the River Tay

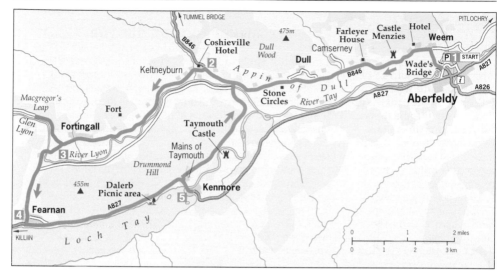

4 🚲 Bear left here on to the A827, towards Aberfeldy. The road hugs the loch shore for about 3 miles (5km), passing Dalerb lochside picnic area and toilets. At the head of the loch follow the road round to the right, to reach the conservation village of Kenmore.

5 🚲 After exploring Kenmore, return across the top of the loch and turn right on to a minor road which continues along the bottom of the hill. Pass the blue-grey mansion of Taymouth Castle off to your right (off-road cycle routes lead off from the left here), and keep straight on. The road bends round to the left; shortly, turn sharp right to cross a girder bridge and meet the B846. Turn right here and retrace the route back along the lovely Tay valley, through Weem to Aberfeldy.

The Black Watch memorial, Aberfeldy, near the bridge

PLACES OF INTEREST

Aberfeldy: The pleasant little town of Aberfeldy, on the River Tay, is a popular touring base for exploring this scenic central part of Scotland. Its most famous feature is the splendid five-arch bridge, which was designed by the great Scottish architect William Adam, but takes its name from the man responsible for its construction, road-builder General Wade. Four obelisks point proudly to the sky from its high parapets.

Two Castles: Two quite different examples of Scottish castles are passed on this route. Castle Menzies (pronounced 'Mingus'), just beyond Weem is a typical Z-plan fortified tower house, dating from the 16th century. Its turbulent history includes a number of military occupations over the centuries, and a fleeting visit by Prince Charles Edward Stuart on his way to Culloden. (Open from April to October.)
Taymouth Castle, near Kenmore, was greatly expanded in the 18th century by its owner, the 1st Earl of Breadalbane (known as 'Slippery John'), who commissioned William Adam to build two wings on to the existing keep. Successive generations made ever more radical alterations, including extensive landscaping of the grounds. The castle passed out of the family in the 1920s, and its more recent history is chequered.

Fortingall: This pretty village near the eastern end of Glen Lyon claims to have the oldest yew tree in Britain standing in its venerable churchyard. A

WHAT TO LOOK OUT FOR

Robert Burns was attracted to this area, and particularly admired the views from Kenmore, and recorded his impressions in verse in the local inn, where they may still be discovered. Look out for a small island in the loch here, too, with the remains of a 12th-century priory.

---

stranger claim is that Pontius Pilate was born here, his father a Roman emissary. There are plenty of early remains here, from prehistoric stone circles to the remains of a medieval homestead, but the Roman link appears tenuous.

Glen Lyon: Stretching for some 25 miles (40km) west toward Killin, Glen Lyon is one of the most scenic glens in Scotland. At its eastern end it is richly wooded, with ancient beech forests covering the steep hillsides of the narrow Pass of Lyon. Macgregor's Leap is named after Gregor MacGregor, who supposedly jumped across the river here to escape pursuers in the mid-16th century; he was later caught and executed on the site of nearby Taymouth Castle.

Castle Menzies is a typical fortified Z-plan tower house

RIDE 46
GRAMPIAN
NO697954

Banchory

This scenic route follows the Dee, one of the world's most famous salmon rivers, and calls in at the fine castles of Drum and Crathes. To avoid the hills, sections of the route are on main roads which may be busy at peak times; a quieter stretch runs along the line of a dismantled railway.

INFORMATION

Total Distance
25 miles (40km),
with 3 miles (5km) off-road

Grade
2

The spectacular Falls of Feugh

OS Map
Landranger 1:50,000 sheet 38
(Aberdeen)

Tourist Information
Banchory (summer), tel: 01330 822000

Cycle Shops/Hire
Monster Bikes, Banchory,
tel: 01330 825313

Nearest Railway Station
Aberdeen (18 miles/29km);
Stonehaven (16 miles/25.5km)

Refreshments
Several hotels and cafés in Banchory;
on the route, options include The
Irvine Arms at Drumoak, a tea room at
Drum Castle and a licensed restaurant
at Crathes Castle

START & ROUTE DIRECTIONS

Start

The little town of Banchory lies 18 miles (29km) west of Aberdeen, on the A93. Begin the ride from Bellfield car park (free) on the east side of the B974, close to the junction with the A93.

Directions

[1] From the car park turn left on to the B974, cross the River Dee and in ½ mile (1km) turn left, signed to Durris. Cross the Bridge of Feugh, and proceed for 3½ miles (5.5km) along the south side of the Dee valley to reach a junction with the A957.

Banchory, with the Hill of Fare behind

[2] Turn right and immediately left and stay on the B9077 for a further 3½ miles (5.5km), passing through Kirkton of Durris. At the crossroads turn left, signposted to Park. Cross the River Dee by Park Bridge, and continue up to meet the A93 at Drumoak. Turn right here, signposted to Aberdeen.

The extensive mansion of Drum Castle stems from an old square keep

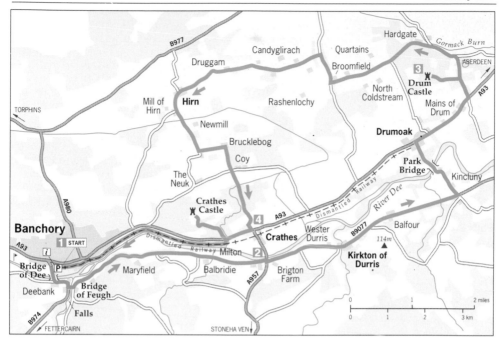

After 1½ miles (2.5km) turn left, signposted 'Drum Castle', and then take the first turning left into the Drum Castle estate. Continue on this lane to reach Drum Castle.

③ ♻ Return to the public road and turn left by a notice pointing to Cullerlie Stone Circle. After ½ mile (1km) turn left and after a further ½ mile (1km) keep left (both junctions are without signposts). Continue for 2 miles (3km) and at the Rashenlochy notice, turn right. In ½ mile (1km) turn left, signposted to Hirn. Keep straight on for 2½ miles (4km) to Hirn and keep left twice – the second junction is signposted to Crathes. Follow the signs to Crathes, turning sharply left and then right, and go straight on at a minor

crossroads to reach a junction with the A93.

④ ♻ Turn right on to the A93 (no signpost) heading west towards Banchory. After ½ mile (1km) turn right into Crathes Castle estate, taking extreme care because of high vehicle speeds and poor visibility. (*Note:* road alterations, including better access to The Old Railway Line, a restaurant and information centre are

The Bridge of Feugh

planned at the entrance to Crathes, so the road layout may change.) Return down the estate road. Immediately before the A93, turn left on an unsurfaced track, following a notice to Crathes Craft Studios. Pass under the main road and turn immediately right on the path which leads up to the old railway line. Continue on this track for 3 miles (5km) into Banchory. On your way, at a wood yard, there is a locked gate (to prevent motor vehicles using this route) which you have to walk around. Reach a tarred path, and go forward through the park keeping the houses on your right. Turn left on the path to pass under the old railway bridge, and continue through Bellfield Park to return to the car park.

PLACES OF INTEREST

Banchory: Banchory is a small town in the lower valley of the River Dee with a sunny aspect and a fine golf course beside the river. The great composer for the fiddle, James Scott Skinner was born here in 1843, and a memorial to 'the Strathspey King' stands on the High Street. For keen off-road cyclists, there is a trail in nearby Blackhall Forest.

Park Bridge: This was originally a toll bridge built to bring customers from the south side of the River Dee to the railway. The bridge is high above the water and provides excellent views. Downstream on the north side of the river there is a football pitch with picnic tables by the river bank.

Drum Castle and Garden: The magnificent castle of Drum combines a 13th-century square tower with a Jacobean mansion house with fine furniture and paintings. The castle was owned for 653 years by the Irvine family before being taken into the care of the National Trust for Scotland. In the walled garden the Trust has gathered a beautiful collection of historic roses (open daily in summer).

Crathes Castle and Garden: It can come as no surprise that Crathes Castle is one of Scotland's most popular visitor attractions, for it offers a splendid, turreted castle in a beautiful garden setting. The ancestral home of the Burnetts of Leys, it has several features of particular note, including painted ceilings (rediscovered in 1877), a finely carved long gallery, and a unique family treasure, the 'Horn of Leys', an ancient ivory horn presented by Robert the Bruce. (Castle open from April to October.) The garden and grounds (open all year) are well worth exploring – the former is enclosed by a high hedge of yew that is almost 300 years old.

WHAT TO LOOK OUT FOR

The River Dee is fed by melting snow from the high Cairngorm mountains. If you do not see fish leaping the falls in Water of Feugh, whilst on your cycle ride, why not come back on an evening stroll. The fish are mainly Atlantic salmon which return here in the spring and summer to spawn in the river of their birth.
Cross the river on the footbridge to learn more about the life of the salmon from the Tourist Information board at the Falls car park.

The gardens at Crathes

INDEX

(numbers refer to cycle routes)

ACKNOWLEDGEMENTS

The Automobile Association would like to thank the following photographers and libraries for their assistance in the preparation of this book.

D FORSS 4
D HARDLEY 185, 186, 187, 188
J HENDERSON 193, 194a, 194b, 196
RALEIGH INDUSTRIES LTD 5a, 5b, 6a, 6b, 7a, 7b, 8, 9
ZEFA PICTURES LTD Front cover

The remaining pictures are held in the Association's own library (AA PHOTO LIBRARY) with contributions from:
P AITHIE 144; A BAKER 39, 41, 156; P BAKER 26, 28, 56; J BEAZLEY 111b, 147b; M BIRKITT 85, 86, 87a, 87b, 88, 89, 90, 92, 93, 94, 95, 96, 97, 98, 99, 107, 110, 113, 114, 116, 117, 118, 119, 120a, 120b; L BLAKE 212; E BOWNESS 165, 166, 167, 168, 169, 170, 171, 172; P BROWN 65, 67b; I BURGUM 125, 126, 127, 128, 129, 130, 132, 133, 134a, 134b, 136a, 136b; J CARNIE 177, 179a, 179b, 180; S L DAY 29, 30, 32, 34, 35, 36, 45, 47, 48, 49, 50, 51, 52, 101, 102a, 102b; P EDEN 57, 60; D FORSS 67a, 68, 74, 76, 80, 81, 83, 84; V GREAVES 147a; S GREGORY 163; J HENDERSON, 189, 190, 191, 192; A LAWSON 20, 23a, 23b, 43; C LEES 173, 175, 176; S & O MATHEWS 58, 69, 73, 79, 100; R MOSS 13, 15, 16, 17, 19a, 19b, 21, 24, 25, 38, 40, 42, 44; G MUNDY 198; R NEWTON 122; D NOBLE 77, 78; N RAY 104; K PATERSON 181, 183, 184; M SHORT 137; R SURMAN 164; M TRELAWNY 70; A TRYNER 109, 111a; W VOYSEY 53, 54, 55, 61, 63a, 63b, 64, 91; R WEIR 195; J WELSH 105, 106, 108, 121, 123, 124, 138, 140, 141, 143, 145, 148; L WHITWAM 112, 149, 150, 152, 153, 154, 155, 157, 158, 159, 160, 161, 162; H WILLIAMS 33, 37